ASIC F

Raddatz, Fritz Joachim.

The survivor

Discard

**STARK COUNTY
DISTRICT LIBRARY**
CANTON, OHIO 44702

7 day

APR 26 1989

THE SURVIVOR

THE SURVIVOR

A NOVELLA

FRITZ J. RADDATZ

Translated from the German by Ralph Manheim

LITTLE, BROWN AND COMPANY
BOSTON   TORONTO   LONDON

COPYRIGHT © 1984 BY ROWOHLT VERLAG GMBH, REINBEK BEI HAMBURG

ENGLISH-LANGUAGE TRANSLATION COPYRIGHT © 1989 BY RALPH MANHEIM

ALL RIGHTS RESERVED. NO PART OF THIS BOOK MAY BE REPRODUCED IN ANY FORM OR BY ANY ELECTRONIC OR MECHANICAL MEANS, INCLUDING INFORMATION STORAGE AND RETRIEVAL SYSTEMS, WITHOUT PERMISSION IN WRITING FROM THE PUBLISHER, EXCEPT BY A REVIEWER WHO MAY QUOTE BRIEF PASSAGES IN A REVIEW.

FIRST ENGLISH-LANGUAGE EDITION

The characters in this book are fictitious.
Any similarity to real persons, living or dead,
is coincidental and not intended by the author.

Library of Congress Cataloging-in-Publication Data

Raddatz, Fritz Joachim.
  [Kuhauge. English]
  The survivor: a novella / Fritz J. Raddatz; translated from the
German by Ralph Manheim. — 1st English language ed.
      p.   cm.
  Translation of: Kuhauge.
  ISBN 0-316-73213-3
  1. World War, 1939–1945 — Fiction. I. Title.
PT2678.A236S8713 1989   88–23726
833'.914 — dc 19   CIP

10 9 8 7 6 5 4 3 2 1

Designed by Robert G. Lowe

FG

*Published simultaneously in Canada
by Little, Brown & Company (Canada) Limited*

PRINTED IN THE UNITED STATES OF AMERICA

THE SURVIVOR

Coweyes

"Soup Chicken swiped fool's gold, Soup Chicken swiped fool's gold" — ten-year-old Bernd's voice crackled with impish malice as he raced gleefully around the house, denouncing his grandmother, who had stolen a cheap tiepin for him in a department store, a plump gold-plated heart with an imitation ruby in it, fastened to a notched, "hard-to-steal" pin. "Fool's gold" was what he called cheap jewelry, and Bernd's grandmother, the aged widow of a head forester, was dubbed "Soup Chicken" by her daughter, who had a knack for cruel nicknames. The old woman was indeed scrawny, her graying hair had a plucked look, and the way she blinked when teased made her seem to lack eyelids. For years her helpless response to her daughter's teasing was "Oh, Irmchen, dear child." The "dear child" was Irmfried, née Imfelden, briefly Kraft, then Walther.

An attractive redhead, she had gray eyes, strangely rounded at the top, but flat at the bottom, which gave her a lurking, catlike look. She was a "blue angel" from the suburbs, chic in a lower-middle-class way. Her looks and her quick, acid wit had given her entrée to clubs and dances, where she soon succeeded in being taken for a lady. A used-car dealer had supplied her with a house, a BMW cabriolet, large hats, silk stockings with black seams, and countless articles of wearing apparel featuring turquoise, her favorite color. She loved the tea dancing at the Hotel Excelsior on Potsdamer Platz and the Uhland Eck on Kurfürstendamm, where the main attraction was a big black man who helped the ladies out of their coats — when she went there, she consequently liked to wear a black velvet coat with a long zipper at the back. The glass dance floor was given over to the fox-trot and tango. No jazz. Though Berlin-by-night still ignored the war, its frivolities were subject to certain limits. Still, certain entertainers were thought to be "thrilling," and audiences "thrilled" to their inept performances while sipping pink champagne. Rosita Serrano sang, "Red poppy, why must you fade so soon," Heinz Rühmann sang, "Rain drops tapping at my window," and, very rarely, Zarah Leander came out in incredible toilettes and confided with a deep-throated sigh that the wind had sung her a song.

Irmchen's marriage to Kraft, the used-car dealer,

did not last long after bank president Walther appeared on the scene. She became his second wife, Bernd's stepmother. Soup Chicken wasn't really his grandmother, because there's no such thing as a step-grandmother. But "step" she was. And in spite of homemade gooseberry jam and knitted mittens with Norwegian patterns, all made in her furnished room in the suburb of Lichtenrade, Bernd made her feel it.

What "it" was, he couldn't have said. A change of air, but not in the sense of a vacation. Though it had begun during the summer holidays. Some years before, widower Walther had given up the Baltic seaside and taken to spending his vacations on an estate in Westphalia belonging to an industrialist. "Uncle Emil" lived there with a former dancer, a delicately boyish, elegantly dressed woman, whom Bernd ardently admired. It never occurred to him that she was not Uncle Emil's wife but his mistress — until he noticed and asked about the initials E. F. engraved on the key of her red Steyr, to him the most exciting vehicle in the world. She replied: "Those are my initials. My name isn't Scholte, it's Frederikson. Uncle Emil is married to another woman."

That meant little to Bernd — Aunt Erni was there, and that's what mattered. Once in a while she turned up alone in Berlin and came to see his father. Bernd admired her; he loved her smell, her movements, her laugh, and the assurance with which she directed an army of servants on the estate, making enormous pots of currant jelly, raspberry jam, or quince preserves.

This year his father had traveled back and forth a number of times. And then he had taken Bernd for a walk around the lake. That was suspicious, as alarming as calling him by his full name, Bernd-Jörn, which occurred only when Bernd had done something wrong or come home with an unsatisfactory report card. "Bernd-Jörn, would you please come here!" That always announced a beating. In such cases his father usually had someone else summon him, the governess or the maid. The beating he did himself. With an air of thin-lipped self-righteousness, for corporal punishment was one of the basic principles of education. The instrument employed was a horsewhip made of steel covered with a layer of straw and another of leather. Duty and punishment were the twin foundations of the household. Table manners were taught with the same whip, the frayed end of which revealed straw and steel. If Bernd slouched in his chair, his father would pass the whip behind his back and through the crook of his elbows. That made it very hard for Bernd to reach his plate; he could do so only by sitting up straight. That was the Prussian regime in which the pastor's son, cadet, and then officer in the Imperial army had grown to manhood. The external signs of it that had remained were the gray suede gloves, which closed over the wrist with an ivory clasp and covered the hands of Friedrich-Wilhelm Walther like a second skin almost regardless of the weather. He had detested the Weimar Republic, which he identified with "the system," as much as he did his civilian occupation. This he had shown on official holidays by displaying black, white, and red instead of black, red, and gold flags — even on sand castles in Fischerhafen on the Baltic. He protested his unloved civilian status — his luggage was stamped "Major General, Ret.," and he expected his barber, his tailor, and his employees to address him by his military title — by leaving his car in the garage and taking the number nine streetcar to his office in a huge gray nineteenth-century building, on Dönhoffplatz in the inner city, belonging to a film company whose financial director he had become. He took the trip four times a day, to work in the morning, home for lunch, back to the office in the afternoon, and home again in the evening, invariably on the same streetcar line. Meals were punctual and on the scanty side. Roast and dessert only on Sunday; "Glabberjucks," a green or red gelatin dessert with vanilla sauce, hardly ever. When there were cold cuts, only his father got salami and Swiss cheese. Meals were served by the maid. The governess ate at the table with them. At lunch and supper Bernd was sent across the street and through the little park to the bar for a jug of draft beer; the greatest care was needed to keep the foam from blowing away. On Sunday there was Moselle wine. One hot summer day, Bernd, aged seven at the time, went out into the garden without any clothes on and ran back and forth through the spray of the lawn sprinkler; his father, to punish him, had sent him to the bar for beer just as he was, despite his tears and entreaties. On the way back Bernd had hidden behind a rhododendron tree and peed into the beer.

On Sunday morning before the roast, on the dot of eleven, Bernd's father went to the cemetery to visit his wife's grave. He took the car. Both children had to wear white knee stockings and black buckled shoes, Bernd a dark blue knit-good suit that he hated because it "grew with" him, his sister a button-on pleated skirt. Her name was Hermine; she was four years older than Bernd, and she had ash blonde hair. She was known as Püppi and her hair was dyed. Her mother had been blonde, a blonde French woman, whom the pensioned, unemployed officer had met while at the Tattersall riding school in Grunewald. Giving birth to Bernd had killed her. Friedrich-Wilhelm Walther's grief had found expression in Hermine's bleached hair and the Sunday excursion to the cemetery. The grave, surmounted by a weeping angel with outspread wings and a flowing stone ribbon inscribed with the words "Forever Thine," was in good taste: a bit of lawn, a drooping rosebush, and a boulder with a bronze plate inscribed Alice Walther, née Gedat. The date of birth was not quite accurate. She had never confessed to her husband that she, like him, was born in 1889; she had always twisted it into 1898.

To Bernd "mother" was a figment, not a real person. He had no idea what it was to have a mother and gave free rein to wishful imaginings. Now and then, when he was smaller, his father had pointed at an especially bright star in the sky and said: "That's where Mama lives. She sees you clearly, even in the daytime." Her birthday was celebrated as if she were there, except that no presents were given. Flowers were heaped around the picture in the thin silver frame on Bernd's father's desk, there was wine even for lunch, and for supper — for Bernd this was the interesting part of the day — there was fruit salad, made with grapefruit and fresh pineapple; that had been Mama's favorite dish, and because of it, Bernd loved her dearly. But what he loved was an abstraction; the woman in the picture could just as well have been someone else. "This is your mother" was the same sort of reality as the star. His feeling for his mother was a vague longing for something feminine. Little by little, such things as the photograph and the fruit salad took the place of the real woman; through them he took possession of her.

An imposing wardrobe with the dead woman's clothes in it stood like a forbidden shrine in the parental bedroom. Since her death, tightly gathered mauve curtains had been put up behind the arabesques of the art nouveau glass doors, as though to discourage prying eyes. But the keys to the wardrobe, great monstrous things, the symbols of security, were in the locks. Many, many times Bernd had secretly explored that wardrobe, a crime he kept sedulously to himself and the thought of which made his head spin but heightened his perceptions. He crawled into the big wardrobe. It was dark inside and smelled of a perfume that reminded him of those fruit salads; it had the bitterness of the grapefruit and the soapy sweetness of the pineapple. His face and hands grazed the silk materials, the voile, the moiré, dozens of old dresses made of goods unknown to him. Caressing them, he recaptured his dead mother. He slipped into her — he wanted to be her, he wanted somehow to crawl into that strange, remote woman. He moved quietly, cautiously, like an expert burglar. Only his mucous membranes played him false, a quirk that would be with him all his life. Later on, he would speak of this sudden flow of mucus as a nervous cold. Sniffling, he would unwrap the tissue paper from blouses and jumpers, open bottles that had long been empty, strange cases with elbow-length gloves in them, and lacquered boxes containing hats adorned with veils and artificial flowers. The two things that impressed him most were a pair of black silk slippers with high thin heels and paste clips and a salmon-colored evening gown with a long train that must once have been brownish or lavender; the color had paled to an indefinable aubergine, and the dress was hopelessly tattered. It *had* to be — he couldn't have said why he was so sure — it *had* to be his mother's wedding dress. The little boy stepped into the dress and it engulfed him like foaming spray. He was hardly bigger than a sleeve; an ugly childlike gnome, he rose from the frills at the back; the endless brown train dragged behind him, and from somewhere in that river of silk protruded the glittering pointed tips of the black silk slippers. Though barely able to control the flow of nervous mucus, he spun about in an orgiastic dance in front of the big mirror, causing a rip in the whirling fabric. This was his own secret fairy tale, told by his mother's fragile dead gowns.

As he saw it, only creatures who wore such dresses were women. His instinct was as sure as it was warped. Servants didn't count. Ladies who occasionally came to see his father were potential mothers; for pretty young women kept turning up, who made a point of bringing little presents for the well-to-do widower's children. To Bernd this was more than welcome. In that house chocolate was kept under lock and key, and other sweets were a rarity; it took persistent begging to get ten pfennigs for an Eskimo pie out of the retired major general, who occasionally bought himself green rubber animals with the money set aside each month for "ethnic Germans in foreign lands." Even at the children's birthday parties — which regularly ended with a big bowl of lemon custard — the retired major general remained true to his principles. If Bernd began to cry because Anette or Günter had fished out the chocolate cookie, his father would say sternly: "Remember, Bernd, that you are the host." One Easter morning, when Bernd had finally found the lavender Easter eggs in the crocus bed, he had stuffed them both in his mouth for fear of his sister, who was quicker than he — a story often repeated in the family circle to Hermine's delight and Bernd's discomfiture.

The father's ladies had no difficulty in currying favor with the son. "You're my favorite aunt," he would cry out at the sight of a promising little package, and jump up on the visitor's lap. It never occurred to him that the implied comparison might offend the lady and embarrass his father. He would gladly have accepted any of these young women as a new mama.

A new mama — that was exactly what the suspicious walk around Aunt Erni's lake, which had begun with the ominous "Bernd-Jörn," followed by the unprecedented "You see, my son, there's something I want to discuss with you," was all about. After a series of awkward and, as Bernd noted to his surprise, pointless questions about school, one thing that certainly wasn't on his mind in vacation time, Herr Walther suddenly came out with it: "How would you like to have a mother again?" Bernd had no need to think it over; he was delighted. The second question, however, presented a problem. "Have you anyone in mind?" As they proceeded around the lake, Friedrich-Wilhelm Walther was no doubt amused at his son's "manliness" and at the same time horrified by his indiscriminate affection. Bernd's memories of chocolate and marzipan brought forth one name after another, all "favorite aunts." Bernd found his father's objections — "But she's married," "But she's much too young," or "No, she lives in Munich" — rather annoying. Something told him that there was no need to involve him in such problems.

"What would you say to Frau Kraft?" Bernd hadn't even thought of her. She had been to the house three or four times, she had made him a beautiful pair of pajamas, and recently, just before the summer holidays, she had brought him a chocolate cake. Bernd reacted with consternation. "But she's married." "She can get a divorce. I mean, that is, she is getting a divorce." For the first time in his life, the boy felt superior to this father, who, it seemed to him, had never been so unsure of himself. All this traipsing around the lake suddenly struck him as ridiculous. And the questions were not really questions, they were announcements on the order of "We're having roast veal for dinner on Sunday." And imprudently Bernd said as much. "Then it's all settled, I suppose. She seems nice enough, but I don't really know her very well. Anyway, it's all right with me." Somewhat at a loss, not entirely reassured, but visibly relieved at having put a bothersome duty behind him, Bernd's father quickly put an end to the walk and his stay. "You two will take the train back, alone."

Already Hermine knew all about it. Once again their father had told her first. With the self-assurance and infinite condescension of her four years' seniority, she made her reaction known to her little brother. "I said to Papa, I hope you realize, I said, that I will call Frau Kraft Frau Kraft, I won't call her Mummy or Mama, I won't, that's what I said." Silly goose, Bernd thought, that's all she is, a silly goose, like all women at that age. Even he knew that Frau Kraft wouldn't be called Frau Kraft anymore.

As he lay in bed that night, the snot ran out of his nose.

The trip back to Berlin was glorious. Brother and sister had never taken the train by themselves. True, Hermine gave a contemptuous snort and flounced out of the compartment when Bernd, who was incapable of carrying a tune, insisted on piping "Oh why, oh why must I leave town" every time the train pulled out of a station. But on the whole they enjoyed themselves thoroughly, thanks to Aunt Erni's enormous food packages.

Neither of them felt the least uneasiness or special expectation. Words like "marriage" and "new mother" had no precise meaning, they were phantasms like next year's vacation.

Their father was waiting at the Anhalt Station. He took a taxi. Bernd loved these dark green, disproportionately wide and tall cars with a black-and-yellow stripe running all around them, folding seats, and a partition between the driver and his fares; he loved the smell of leather and stale cigarette smoke. But the taxi stopped in front of a strange house.

Richthofenallee. Herr Walther was as proud of the name as if he had given it to the street, for he himself had served in the Richthofen Squadron. It was a short street, bordered by none-too-fashionable row houses grouped in a circle around a former gravel pit, which had been divided up like wedges of cake and converted into gardens. Their owners never called them anything but "houses"; the word "villa" struck them as pretentious and offended their sense of middle-class solidity. Since the death of Bernd's mother, number 17 had remained unchanged inside and out. The ugly brownstone front was covered with Virginia creeper, the shutters were wobbly and crooked, and the dirty gray window guards, in the soft metal of which Bernd had often scratched names and funny faces, had broken loose from the mortar. The garden door squeaked a sort of triad when opened and, oddly enough, a different tune when closed. The whole place had the homey quality of a stopped wall clock — dark furniture, too tall and wide for a modern house; in the dining room a carved black oak buffet, and over the table a silk-shaded lamp, from which, on a twisted cord, hung a small ebony bell with a white button. Dark, old-fashioned wallpaper, lamps whose light was smothered by embroidered Spanish shawls, and in all the rooms threadbare carpets. The curtains, for the most part velvet or satin, were edged with black wooden beads, and the frayed runner on the stairs leading to the upper story, where the bedrooms, children's rooms, and guest rooms were situated, was held in place from step to step by brass rods, every second one of which had broken loose from its moorings.

A house in town had been Alice Gedat's dowry. Until their daughter was born, they had lived in one of the big Berlin apartment houses on Bayerischer Platz. The "new house" had been bought when Bernd was born. Frau Walther had been sickly since then, and they wanted a brighter, sunnier place with a garden. She no longer had the strength to set up a whole new household. The customary surroundings made her feel secure. She had grown up in Paris, in just such houses with just such furniture, and her father, the veterinarian Auguste Gedat, Grampa Auguste, as Bernd called him, was glad on his annual visit to Berlin to find himself in a familiar setting. Each of these visits was an event. Bernd looked forward to them for weeks. The old man lived in retirement in Monte Carlo, where he was cheerfully gambling away his considerable fortune. A huge man with a long beard, a lorgnette, and watch charms on a gold chain, he had a number of ironclad maxims that drove his housekeepers to despair. One of them was "Mondamin* *must* be made with

*A packaged pudding, normally made with no eggs at all.

twelve eggs." Bernd's favorite was "Children *must* eat chocolate puffs." His arrival was regularly celebrated in a little pastry shop by just the two of them, the huge old man and ugly little Bernd, who managed on one occasion to consume a whole dozen of these desirable little pastries, to the delight of his grandfather, who egged him on with: "Geep id up, *mon petit.*" Before lunch the old man smoked cigars; then came his afternoon nap — whenever possible, Bernd stayed in the room to observe the puffing, grunting mountain — after which Grampa Auguste smoked a long meerschaum pipe. While Bernd stuffed, the natural phenomenon named Auguste told wild stories about palm trees, castles that he referred to as casinos, and horse racing. Bernd was far from understanding them, but he savored their sensuous atmosphere. To the maid's indignation, Grampa never used a wallet; his pockets were full of change and wadded bills that fell out when she brushed his clothes. Bernd fingered the old man as he did his mother's dead gowns; the terrain was strangely familiar to him. Bernd's father and one of his mother's brothers who lived in Paris had tried to rescue their inheritance by talking him out of Monte Carlo. So Auguste Gedat had gone to Baden-Baden, suspiciously enough with a nurse, to whom in the end he had bequeathed his entire fortune. Bernd knew nothing about money, but he understood enough of the family's indignation over Grampa Auguste's "betrayal" to be glad that the old man had put one over on them. To Bernd his grandfather was at once a strange continent and a familiar piece of furniture, like the embroidered cockatoos on the dim dark lamp shades. When he died, the house lost a little more of its life; more than ever it became congealed memory. Every attempt by one or another housekeeper to introduce some innovation was stifled by an absent "Yes, yes, you're quite right — we'll see." That was the retired major general's way of defending his sepulcher.

But this was not the house where the taxi stopped. Only the number was still the same. The "house" had become a villa. Gone was the Virginia creeper. The front was now a light gray. The window guards were now of sheet metal, the shutters and mullions black. The neglected front garden, hitherto full of dandelions and French marigolds, had become a cool, close-cropped lawn. The new, black garden gate no longer gave off music. The highly polished letter slots and nameplates looked entirely different.

Neither of the children said a word. They wiped their feet and boarded the strange, spruce ship. It wasn't theirs anymore. The white walls, the light-colored carpeting in the entrance, the hallway, and all the ground-floor rooms made everything look twice as big as before. Palms and large potted plants. Everything was oblique. This was the rectilinear style that later became known as art deco: functional, cold, and geometrical. In the dining room the ponderous buffet had been replaced by a "sideboard" covered with whitish sharkskin surmounted by severe silver candlesticks. The curtains were of beige damask. The bell for the servants was hidden under the carpet. The living room had become a drawing room: groups of low chairs, flower arrangements, and an enormous phonograph. Instead of the old knickknacks, crystal bowls, and *bonbonnières*, plain rectilinear objects: folding ashtrays, cocktail shakers, a Lalique punch bowl. For Bernd every door in the house had had its face, characteristic of the room behind it: a certain position of the key, a slight inclination of the handle, on some doors a clamp that held the key in place. There had been grinning doors and sad ones, some had been menacing, others had seemed to smack their lips; some had been capricious, changeable. But every one had had a familiar expression. The door to his father's study had always reminded him of a seal, sometimes twinkling merrily and sometimes exceedingly threatening. Now there were no door handles or locks — only octagonal, chrome-plated knobs. A fist had shattered their faces.

"Welcome home, children," said a voice from the sliding glass door between the drawing room and the study. "I'm so glad you're here. We're sure to get along swimmingly, we'll be a real family. I married your papa last week."

"Good evening, Frau Kraft," said the Bitch. Bernd didn't know what was expected of him. Father wasn't there — there was only his room, the library, behind the lady in a turquoise tunic. Father's study could be entered only in emergencies, when "Bernd-Jörn" was summoned, when report cards were to be shown, or a visiting stranger was to be politely announced. Hesitantly, he approached the strange woman. Suddenly he was seized with an impulse to jump up and kiss her. She caught him like a big ball. In that instant he glimpsed her again, this time in the narrow silver frame on his father's desk, in color, with bangs. She had a striped dress and she was smiling. Bernd's kiss skidded. "Clumsy little rascal," she said, patting him on the behind. "And now we're going to celebrate. I've baked you a cake for dinner. And you'll get chocolate, Coweyes. That's what I'm going to call you from now on. What absurdly big eyes you have!"

A House with False Eyelashes

The wind, the current, the climate had changed, and the ship, the *Yuricke,* as Irmchen, who knew her Traven, called the house, was taking a new course. Irmchen was given to nicknames. She felt that they transformed things and people into something strange. She called the maid "the Bomb," because of the breakage; Hermine was "the Snail," because she was so lazy and slow-moving; her general term for children was "Reptile," and she called her husband "Wotan," because of his towering rages.

The rages stopped. This was the greatest change that Bernd noticed. "Good riddance," as "Irmchen, dear child" put it — all of a sudden, Father wasn't there anymore. No more beatings. No more being sent out for beer. No more visits to the weeping stone angel. The crew of the *Yuricke* were no longer the same. The house had been more than done over

— its new mistress had a way of carrying things too far. She was determined to turn the mere house into a villa. The parts of it that were too small for a villa — the stairwell, for instance — had to be enlarged by means of wall mirrors and sophisticated lighting effects. A house with false eyelashes. She would never have thought of removing the previous owner's coronets from the door of her car, an ancient, dark green Horch — a "little gift," as she called semi-purloined objects. And she had changed her maiden name of Imfelden, inherited from a long line of foresters, to Im Felden, which somehow suggested nobility.

She seemed to have rarefied the air in the house. The father and his two children no longer lived together. The family law had become betrayal. Hermine's betrayal was the most painful.

There had been no rapport between them as children. Long years had passed since Hermine had sung: "Dear stork, I beg on bended knee, A little brother bring to me." Four years younger than herself, little brother had soon become a tiresome toy; they had never played together. But Bernd had always had a weakness for her playthings, especially her dolls. The most stunning armored cars, even Adolf Hitler with upraised arm in an open Mercedes with real rubber tires and a spare wheel, lay idle when he was able to get hold of a doll. Unfortunately, he always broke it — soon wood-shaving intestines would be hanging out, a porcelain eye would be gone, or the belly-voice would fall silent. Hermine thought it normal that this should bring a beating at the end of the day. She had a simple rule of life: in this world there is a certain quantity of beatings — or of cake, for that matter. The more one person got, the less would be left for another. Where beatings were concerned, she made sure that Bernd would get the lion's share. With cake it was the other way around.

This required no great effort on her part, because their father idolized her. When in the course of their Sunday visit to the cemetery she would whimper, "Baby had enough" and sit down obstinately in a clump of ferns, he would pick her up and carry her. She regularly got the larger portion of dessert — a heartbreaking business. Bernd's first diary began with the lament: "She got two helpings of Glabberjucks." During one of the most rabid beatings, this time with the flexible plaited dog whip, she slid down the banister, shrieking jubilantly: "We're going to Jerusalem and Bernd-Jörn is *not* invited." His offense: he had crept up to the dark attic next door to the maid's room, where his father kept his old uniforms in a mahogany chest. A coffin. An armory full of spiked helmets, horse's tails, sabers, and blue-and-white uniform cloth. It was a spooky, exciting room, the rough unplaned beams sprayed sparks if you rubbed furiously against them, and the wardrobe was a cabinet of smells — moth flakes, leather, and rust. Bernd's friends had organized a "platoon" in the park and he was determined to be the top brass, so he had cut off the buttons, braid, and epaulets with a razor blade filched from the bathroom and sewn them on an old tracksuit. When months later his father, on the occasion of his annual moth hunt, discovered the crime, he was beside himself with rage. The razor blade in his son's hand had cut into his very flesh. This beating had been carried out with almost homicidal frenzy. Hermine had squealed with delight.

"Irmchen, dear child" took to courting her stepdaughter. Obviously Coweyes counted for little with her newly acquired husband. But the Snail had to be coaxed out of her shell and turned in the right direction. She was the dead wife, whose power had to be neutralized if Irmchen's conquest of the husband was to be complete.

Irmchen founded a corporation that she called "we." Its shares were little phrases: We women. You and I. Irmchen and Hermine. What are men good for? Let Wotan split a gut. Let Coweyes go to the market and stand in line for cabbage. We'll spend the afternoon at the KDW department store. There's a movie opening tomorrow at the Ufa-Palast am Zoo. *Auf Wiedersehen Franziska* with Marianne Hoppe. We. Ice cream and cake at Kempinski's. Irmchen and Hermine. Stockings. Fancy shoes. Giggle together behind discreet hands. Fashion show at the Excelsior. Fatherland House.* Moselle section. Hairdresser's. Hermine now had a function. Budding socialite. They rehearsed for weeks. The opening night was a big success.

The new lady of the house gave a party once a month. That was in 1942. The year in which Auschwitz and Maidanek opened for business. Irmchen served "Swedish cup," always a big hit now that everything was in short supply.

There were usually about twenty guests, a few dashing officers, an architect and wife, a banker or two, a Sarotti† executive. Bernd wasn't allowed to attend. A fairy carnival. Already in pajamas, secretly, hidden behind a curtain, he looked on, peering through the gaps between the banister supports: furs, perfume, fashionable women, laughter, music, and most painful of all, great trays full of canapés. Culminating in the shout of triumph: "And now I'll make you all a Swedish cup." Hermine was always there. The mixture of preserved fruit, water ice, and ersatz whipped cream was served in champagne glasses. Then came green cocktails, a specialty of Irmchen's. Once Bernd, maddened by desire, had crept down to the kitchen and licked the sticky, more-or-less-empty glasses. When caught, he wasn't

---

Haus Vaterland. An entertainment center with rooms decorated in the style of various picturesque places — Egypt, Naples, the Moselle Valley, etc.

†A well-known brand of chocolate.

beaten, but to his surprise and consternation driven into the candlelit, strangely fragrant living room and made to bow to all the fairy princesses, who laughed at the sight of his big round jack-o'-lantern head with its bulging eyes and protruding ears, perched on a scrawny little body in striped flannel pajamas. The room spun around. He stumbled into one of the coveted trays and was chased upstairs like a wayward goose — "That Coweyes, he's really *too* stupid."

But this was to be a special, gala party. The house was all aflutter. Hermine hadn't been seen since lunchtime. Irmchen was making phone call after phone call. In the late afternoon she began to try on dresses. Early that morning, before going to school, Coweyes had been sent to market for "trimmings": gherkins, sweetening, R. 6 and Muratti cigarettes — Irmchen kept remembering something she had forgotten. She finally decided on a chiffon dress with a wide, silvery belt decorated with sequins. She prevailed on Wotan to pin his little decoration on his lapel. And just before the first guests appeared Bernd saw that Irmchen was wearing his mother's brooch, large opals arranged like flower petals. Bernd was allowed to stay up and wait on the guests. His father was even more irritable than usual. "Where in God's name is Hermine?" "Oh, Wotan, stop grumbling! She'll be here any minute." "Would you kindly tell me where she is? Roaming around in the pitch darkness!" "Don't bother me. Go and see if there's enough sugar for the May wine." Irmchen and Wotan bicker and snap at each other; neither knows why the other is so jumpy. Irmchen wants to try out the records she has bought for the party. "All right. But just the gramophone, please. No radio." "Are you out of your mind? What's got into you? Stop giving me orders! This isn't an army post." The arrival of the first guests forces a pause in the hostilities. Bernd is in seventh heaven, he loves playing the waiter, and best of all, he doesn't have to go to bed. The bell keeps ringing, the door opens and closes, wraps are removed. Bernd watches like a hawk. But the entrance of a ravishing young woman has escaped him. Black hair, a lavender gown with a long zipper in back. It looks familiar, reminds him of the velvet coat his stepmother wore to the Uhland Eck. Yes, it's Irmchen's dress all right. No, yes, oh my God, it's his sister Hermine with her hair dyed black. Irmchen's revenge whirs through the air like an arrow. Wotan, who doesn't smoke, reaches for a cigar. There stands Hermine, a ravishing young lady in one of Irmchen's dresses, a total stranger to him. "Doesn't she look marvelous?" Irmchen asks the company at large, and all those who knew Hermine answer: "Wonderful!" "Incredible!" "A young lady!" "Get that wig off your head this minute!" is Wotan's strangely feeble command, the best he can do. But it's not a wig and her hair has not been dyed. It's just Hermine's natural dark brown hair that has been debleached. Alice Gedat's blondeness has been demolished. Because he's the host, Wotan is unable to bluster. So he gets drunk. Taking advantage of the confusion, Bernd disappears. He crawls into a corner beside the enormous gramophone. "A hundred six, a hundred seven, even now it feels like heaven," sings Heinz Rühmann. Irmchen — always her most effective ploy — has changed her dress again, her way of triumphing over all the other ladies. Now she is wearing a tight-fitting orange velvet dress — she calls it her "standing-up dress" — which contrasts unpleasantly with her red hair, her black elbow-length gloves, and her black feather boa, which reaches to the floor. She knows this is Wotan's favorite dress, she wants to provoke him, to savor her triumph. Bernd falls asleep on the carpet, a young animal that has taken a sip of liqueur. His father's bellowing wakes him up. "Didn't I tell you no radio tonight? Didn't I tell you a thousand times not to turn on the radio?" What with the clatter of glasses and crockery, the laughing fox-trotters, and his father's outburst, which sounds even more hysterical than usual, Bernd is able to catch only a few unfamiliar words — Heydrich, Protector, revenge, Lidice.* "Stupid Coweyes, get to bed." Irmchen's eyes narrow, her winning cards are slipping out of her hand.

*Reinhard Heydrich, Deputy Chief of the Gestapo, then "Reich Protector" of occupied Czechoslovakia, had just been assassinated. In reprisal the Nazis destroyed the Czech village of Lidice (June 9–10, 1942), killing the entire male population.

Much, much later that night Bernd wakes up; the hatred and fear in his father's outburst have taken hold of him. He's shivering. In his mind the fairy princesses are grimacing, the whole party congeals into a ghoulish picture book: his mother's brooch; Irmchen has never done that before; the black-haired Hermine; the tinny radio voice that cut everything to pieces. Bernd has discovered a trick: how to open his room door with a drop of the oil that came with his toy tank. All is still in the house. He creeps down the stairs. An irresistible force impels him to take another look at the deserted rooms; maybe there are still leftovers, glasses that haven't been quite emptied, a piece of apricot cake, or a forgotten "potiphar," as Irmchen calls those little square cookies. A room door is open, a light is still on, the sliding glass door to the living room is closed. He's about to open it when he sees silhouettes through the glass, figures moving silently back and forth on the big divan. His nose begins to run. He snuffles, he's frightened. He can't be sure. But it seems to be his father, Irmchen, and another woman.

In the morning no one wakes him. It's pretty late when his stepmother announces: "You don't have to go to school today. I'll write a note for you. We've got an idea. We're going to play ship. The Snail and I are the passengers, you'll wait on us. Anyway, Papa has forbidden Hermine to go to school with that hair." The two of them, Irmchen and Hermine, lie in the marriage beds. Irmchen shows Hermine how to varnish her nails, and tells her she must never scratch between her toes, "because that makes it worse."

Bernd turned into a rat. You had to be quick. That was what counted. He stole whatever he could find — bits and pieces of soap, sugar, cigarette coupons that he sold to older boys in school. He ran around in old, raggedly patched clothes. His favorite teacher took him aside and asked if that had to be. At school he managed by cheating, copying, and prompting. The only subjects he liked were history and painting. He hated the war books his father gave him; in bed at night he read *Sigismund Rüstig** and *Robinson Crusoe* under the covers with the help of his "flak searchlight." The more exotic, the more remote, the better. He was a year and a half younger than his classmates. When barely five he had begged and pleaded until his father consented to send him to school. Consequently, a good deal of what his classmates said and thought was over his head. A note was passed around the class, and he copied it without thinking. "A cunt lay down upon the beach, to give herself a sunning, Pretty soon a prick came running. He thought he'd fuck the peach." Bernd had left the piece of brown wrapping paper in his toy

---

*Evidently a German adaptation of an adventure story by Captain Frederick Marryatt.

chest. A school friend of his was a druggist's son. One day he swiped some condoms and took them to school. With nothing special in mind, the two boys had played with them. In the end they peed into them, tied them up, and tossed them down into the street. Bernd greeted his classmates' jingles and drawings with enthusiasm, but he never knew exactly what they meant. There was a dictionary in his father's locked bookcase. Bernd knew where the key was hidden, because once, just before Christmas, Wotan, while talking about his battle wounds, had opened his desk drawer and taken out two big sawtooth knives known as bayonets. They were covered with dark spots. "See, this is where a Russian almost ripped my chest open. But I did for *him*. This is my bayonet, the one I killed him with, and these spots are his blood. They don't wash off. You can take my word for it, that swine has gone to a better world. And this case has Mama's jewels in it. I'll give them to Hermine when the time comes." After putting the jewel case down on the desk beside his coffee set, he had taken several keys out of the desk drawer. He'd been sitting in one of the heavy brown armchairs under the death mask of Frederick the Great flanked by two pairs of long, crossed sabers. Bernd didn't care for the jewels, which were supposed to have been so expensive. And the bloody-toothed knives made him retch.

One afternoon while Irmchen and the Snail were out shopping Bernd had filched the keys. But there was no cunt or fuck or prick in the dictionary — there were folding pictures of men and women; they had black lungs and red hearts and blue muscles, but no inkling of what Bernd was looking for. In one of the books he found an envelope with nude pictures of his stepmother. That was boring; he'd seen her through the open bathroom door. The expedition was a failure. He was still as ignorant as ever.

One night his father came into Bernd's room, holding the scribbled slip of paper. Bernd was so amazed at his father's intrusion into his toy chest that he forgot to be afraid. "Do you often write this kind of stuff?" He sounded surprisingly calm; there seemed to be no beatings in the air. His next, strangely friendly question was: "Do you know what it means?" "Well," said Bernd. "As a matter of fact . . . yes, I think . . . no, to tell the truth, I don't." "Stop stuttering. Better forget that stuff. I'll just tear this up." Bernd lay there in a fog of bewilderment and fell asleep.

He awoke in the middle of the night. His father was standing there in his dressing gown. "Come with me, son." Giddy, drunk with sleep, Bernd got up. The door between his room and the parental bedroom had always been locked. But Wotan had come through that door. A lamp was burning in the parental bedroom. Irmchen was lying on the bed naked. Wotan took off his dressing gown. He too was naked.

Once last summer Bernd had looked down from

the upstairs toilet and watched his father in the garden. He had been cutting the daisies out of the lawn with a kitchen knife, to stop them from flowering. Bernd had hidden in this toilet because he detested that sort of work. Squatting there in old blue swimming trunks with a white rubber belt, Wotan was stabbing at the grass. A big brown wrinkled potato was dangling from between his legs. Bernd was interested, but it made him feel sick.

The bedroom that night smells of dried daisies. And bitter almonds. Wotan's body — his chest, his belly, and down to his legs — is matted with black hair. A huge brownish purple post is sticking out of the big wrinkled potato — a weird thing, half animal, half implement — Bernd doesn't know what it is. He is dead-tired, three-quarters asleep, half-dreaming. He feels nothing at all. "All right, Bernd-Jörn. Take off your pajamas. Are you getting hair?" The "Bernd-Jörn" frightens him awake. His striped flannel pants lie in a heap on the carpet. "You're a big boy now — writing such stuff — I'd better show you what it means." Bernd remembers the slip of paper and his father's strange behavior. But what has this got to do with it? How and why and for what is he to be punished? "Come, lie down here, I'll show you how it's done." With an abrupt but somehow incredibly slow movement the huge post disappears. Bernd is supposed to do the same, but he doesn't know how. He feels something viscous and wet, something horribly slippery, and recoils. His stepmother laughs. "Come on, show him, he's only a kid." With her fingers she holds her vagina open. Once, while visiting Aunt Erni on the farm, Bernd had watched the cook cleaning a chicken, cutting through the yellowish white layer of fat. He doesn't see why his stepmother should want to hurt herself. She moans. "See, sonny, this is the way. Like this." All of a sudden the wrinkled potato-thing is dangling between Irmchen's legs, growing out of her. Now she has black hairy legs. And Wotan has a red mop. Soft white arms flow from his shoulders. At the same time his other, hairy arms grab hold of the cowering Bernd. "Don't do anything to yourself," says Wotan breathlessly. "Anything but that. But you can hold mine if you like, to show you what yours will be like someday. There, that's it. But not so tight, move your hands a bit. That's right." The post jumps, it escapes from Bernd's hand, it's much too big for him to hold. Now Wotan is standing next to the bed with his side to the big mirror. "All right. Let's try it again, dumb kid. You've got to sink right in." Bernd sinks into the chicken; it's blubbery, infinitely wet, the hair tickles, the bitter almond smell gets stronger. "You've got to move, son. Don't just cling, that won't get you anywhere." Bernd moves. From deep dark mud he rises to the surface but the waves break over him he's as heavy as lead and as light as a cloud the dead daisies stink and grin and the chicken runs away fluttering the headless chicken keeps on running smooth doughy chicken with hairy black legs red mop pale wings black wings wrinkledpotatochicken stuffed with bitter almonds head bursts mirror bursts ohmyGod she's eating his post. Bernd throws up. Vomits on the post-eating head.

Evacuated

The city was moldering in a brownish early-spring day when Bernd arrived in Görlitz. The Snail had been there for several months; Herr Walther had arranged for her to stay with a woman who had once been her governess. Görlitz was no more than an overgrown market town with a bloated administration. On weekends it was inundated by shoppers: peasants from the country roundabout and miners from the nearby coal fields. The brackish, lazily flowing Neisse provided teenagers with a handy rhyme for *Scheisse* (shit), and the Landeskrone, which the locals thought of as a mountain, was an ideal playground with its gulches, forest trails, and gravel paths. At the Ufa Cinema near the railroad station, streaky, flickering old copies of *Homeland* or *Stukas* or *Ride for Germany* could be enjoyed free of charge by youngsters under sixteen. The boys collected postcards of Zarah Leander, Carl Raddatz, or Willy Birgel; the girls preferred René Deltgen.

In the inner city there was an "Arcade," a pathetic imitation of the glass-roofed marvels of Berlin. The Café Hindenburg served ersatz coffee and bread coated with ersatz liver sausage or butterless shortbread. Toward nightfall the city — including the Arcade, the barber shop, the window of which featured a wax bust with mustache holder, and the Bata shoe store with its oversupply of plastic sandals — was blacked out. That was the hour of the phosphorescent children, invisible except for the luminous Winter Aid badges pinned to their jackets or sweaters — greenish yellow gulls in flight, spotted beetles, or tiny Messerschmidt pursuit planes, as bright as in the beam of a flak searchlight. The Hitler Youth badge was despised as a mere reflector. Oddly enough, only the boys wore these phosphorescent buttons. The girls didn't twinkle. This inspired the boys to invent a special weapon. Made of plywood, it looked like a pistol; the barrel was lined with the rubbing surfaces of matchboxes; matches were propelled through this miniflamethrower by a rubber-band mechanism. The favored target was girls' hair, regardless whether blonde or brunette. Flamethrower expeditions were known as "shooting bees," and the marksman who created the most giggles and screams was the victor of the day.

Night brought a different kind of shooting. Twelve boys in each class were assigned to night duty. They slept on cots in the attic of the schoolhouse. When there was an air raid, they set to work with pails of water, rags, and sandbags to save the hated brick building. The one who finished first was rewarded with a slice of bread and lard, payable the following morning. For Bernd this was a calamity: in the eyes of his school friends, he was the model of excellence in all things — they failed to realize that he was two years younger than they, quicker perhaps and more daring, but much more ignorant and physically above all a lot less mature. Bernd jerked off quicker, better, farther. Anybody knew that. With the same certainty as when he had explained to his football friends that babies came out of the belly button, he knew it for sure, that's the way it was in Berlin, and with his vivid descriptions of the city burning after air raids, he was under obligation to shoot first here. It was expected of him and that was that; take it out and no nonsense. In the fifteen-year-old class he wouldn't have made it — some had already been drafted as antiaircraft auxiliaries. The bread and lard was the finishing tape — the gang would have despised him if he hadn't come in first.

His landlords helped him achieve the indispensable victories. His father had lodged him with a childless pair, Colonel Bauschan (ret.) and his wife, Edelgard, who looked enthroned even when standing, invariably clad in rustling black silk with little white ruffles under her double chin, a woman already widowed during her husband's lifetime. Her attire was as simple as it was statuesque, stiff waxed taffeta, whose crackling pleats shimmered like moiré, with enormous rustling sleeves that obliged her to wear capes rather than coats.

But she had little need of outdoor clothing. She seldom left the house, where she lived as in a mausoleum. Its inhabitants were her dead. Their names were Verdun, Somme, Ypres, and Marne: stuffed glass-eyed white terriers in their baskets lined with striped batiste, each with his nose in an empty dish, beside which lay a greenish blue rubber bone. The colonel had fought in these battles; the terriers were his First World War dead, which, expertly stuffed, had survived the black, red, and gold flag and the swastika, the Weimar Republic and the Third Reich. Over each little basket hung a picture representing one of those memorable battles, each with a black, white, and red ribbon looped around it.

The incumbent terrier bore the name of Stalingrad. He seemed identical with the stuffed basket-heroes, except that he was alive. His masters referred to him as "the poor little animal." When it was time for his dinner: "Where is the poor little animal?" Or when Gertrude the maid was ready to take him out shopping: "Now it's time for the poor little animal to . . ." Gertrude enjoyed neither activity, neither shopping nor taking "the poor little animal" out. The one thing she enjoyed was flying back and forth and up and down on a swing suspended from the high ceiling of the dingy dark corridor. She had nothing on under her skirt, and the great black clump of hair that Bernd saw swinging over his head helped him at night when competing for the bread and lard.

Stalingrad had other interests. The evening meal was eaten punctually at a round table covered with a white filigree tablecloth on top of a green felt mat. On the exact middle of the table stood a lamp skirted in blue-and-orange chintz. Its feeble light fell on a small ebony bell with a black cord. Both the chintz skirt and the bell reminded Bernd of the swinging clump of hair. After dinner, Stalingrad began to whimper, more or less urgently according to what there had been for dinner; if it was jacket potatoes with curds, he didn't stir. If it was muffins and blueberries, the front also remained quiet. A thin piping sound issued from under the table when there was cheese. "The poor little animal doesn't like cheese," said Herr and Frau Colonel in unison. Herr Colonel would then reach under the blue-and-orange chintz skirt for the ebony bell.

Everyone knew that the opposite was true. Stalingrad's whimper grew more penetrating — "the poor little animal" was demanding his right. The table was cleared; Bernd had to sit over the green felt mat, learning amo amas amat. He didn't seem to remember the passive form, meaning "he is loved." Frau Edelgard sat in her wing chair with footrests, reading

Das Reich. She adored poetry. Colonel Bauschan lay on the sofa with a cigar. He had cadged the tobacco coupons in exchange for a cord of illegally cut wood from a forest belonging to him. He had taken his shoes off. This was Stalingrad's moment. With the dexterity of a skirted, tango-dancing poodle in a circus, "the poor little animal" grasped the colonel's socks between teeth and paws and pulled them off. Cheesy white feet, size eleven, emerged from long grayish white underdrawers that had survived Verdun, the Somme, Ypres, and the Marne. They were Stalingrad's delight. "The poor little animal" licked the corns and calluses, the yellowish ingrown toenails, the athlete's foot. Frau Colonel read her book. She had tuned in on the People's Station and turned the "request program" very low; Ilse Werner's voice came piping out of the "people's receiving set." Bernd conjugated amo amas amat. And so did Stalingrad. His agitation mounted as he licked, his pointed little member sprouted bright red from his white fur, his hairless, bluish scrotum grew firm and hard. Evening after evening this performance went on until Frau Edelgard interrupted it with her "Really, Eduard, I ask you." Eduard's cigar had gone out when exactly half consumed. Pleasures must be budgeted. "The poor little animal," he said. "What else can he do?" By then the panting Stalingrad had wedged himself between the colonel's two big toes. Back arched, teeth bared, glassy-eyed like the heroes in the drawing room next door, but whimpering frantically and jerking desperately back and forth, flying as on the swing in the dark corridor. At that point nothing could have stopped him. It never took very long. When Stalingrad was extinguished, Colonel Bauschan took an old kitchen towel. And then Bernd remembered: "amatur."

Front-Line City

The house seemed lifeless and somehow resentful — it ceased to fulfill its function. It said: Why bother for just the two of you? It's beneath me. The potted plants withered, their leaves drooped, the mirrors lost their sheen, the little box behind the kitchen door — originally designed to tell the servants, by displaying little disks marked "dining room," "library," and so forth, in the little window, in what room someone had rung — went on strike. The only disk it showed now said "parents' bedroom." There had never been parents in this house, a "parents' bedroom" existed only in the bell box. The rooms were all out of kilter; the doorknobs had aged, their spotted chrome features were drawn, the heavy ashtrays with the leather straps weighted at the ends to keep them balanced on the chair arms slipped and no longer hid the cracks in the dark brown leather;

the slender white cachepots still stood between the double windows, they still had bowls of water under them, but some had sprung cracks, and there were no hyacinths flowering in them as usual in February. Bernd spent his days in unremitting struggle against the uncooperative house, the furnace that was always going out because of too much or too little coke, or the squeaking blinds with the frayed cords that were always getting stuck.

The two of them, Friedrich-Wilhelm, the father, and his redheaded son, were all alone in the house. No one polished the floors or furniture, no one dusted, no one cleaned the originally yellowish but later dark brown candlesticks on the sideboard, whose sharkskin cover was flaking. The female members of the crew had deserted the *Yuricke* — the Snail refused to run away from the Russians, who were coming closer and closer to Görlitz, and "Irmchen, dear child" was somewhere in the country outside Berlin, keeping away from the bombs, as she put it.

Herr Walther had gotten into the habit of visiting her there on weekends — when she let him, for Bernd often overheard animated telephone conversations in which Irmchen intimated that the next weekend didn't suit her. There was something baffling about these phone calls. Wotan stormed and pleaded by turns; he would issue orders and then a moment later he would be whimpering like a beaten dog.

Sometimes Bernd had to go along on these trips. Especially when the trip, which was far from negligible, had to be taken by bicycle, for by that time few civilians were admitted to the trains. Bernd enjoyed these expeditions. Few of his evacuated classmates had returned, and this was a change from his friendless and schoolless existence. He was a much stronger cyclist than his father, who puffed and panted on every hill, and he took pleasure in his manifest superiority. He was the proud owner of a racing bike with underslung handlebars, which had formerly belonged to "Piggy." Piggy was also known as "the Pimp" because of his long hair and tailored white linen jackets. Accredited with the most daring exploits, he was the admired ringleader of a teenage gang, who eschewed the spit and polish of the HY,* dressed with studied sloppiness, and affected rolled-up leather trousers. Envied and admired by Bernd, who was a year younger, Piggy had everything a teenager could desire. He was strong and fearless, he made no secret of his smoking, he could jump off a moving bicycle, run after it, and jump on again, he had hockey skates with shoes attached, and above all he had a girlfriend — the Snail. She usually took her brother along when she went to meet Piggy in the park — then Bernd would get the bike and race around on it for an hour or two, during which time he dreamed of owning tailored linen jackets and be-

*German HJ, *Hitlerjugend* (Hitler Youth).

ing like Piggy. When Piggy turned eighteen and was drafted, he said to Bernd: "If I'm killed, you can have the bike." Then they had gone to the movies together and Bernd had smoked his first cigarette in the john — his farewell to Piggy. Piggy taught him how to do it: "Don't puff. Pull. Just inhale the smoke and say aloud, 'I'm going to Brandenburg and back'; by the time you say 'back,' the smoke will be in." Never had Bernd been so sick. He never did get to see that movie.

Nor get to see Piggy again. When the card came from Kurland, it wasn't long before all the kids in the neighborhood knew. Bernd had often called for Piggy at his mother's, because no one was supposed to know about Piggy's evening walks with Hermine. Now he went back again. The woman got on his nerves with her tears and lamentations: "He had such beautiful hair; I always washed it in camomile tea" and "He was always first at backstroke." Bernd only said: "The bicycle. He promised me his bicycle." And waited imperturbably while the poor woman, shattered by the death of her only son, shuffled down to the basement and dragged out the gleaming, miraculous bike. Looking down from her balcony, she saw Bernd whizzing happily away through Kurland.

On this bicycle he was now riding to Irmchen's country retreat, his father trailing behind him. Now Bernd was Piggy, Piggy the Strong. As brazenly as though stealing apples from an orchard, Bernd had stolen his dead friend's strength; along with the bicycle, he had appropriated Piggy's attitude of easy superiority: a borrowed, inherited freedom compounded of steel, chrome, and rubber. He rode no-handed. At the top of a long hill he stopped to wait for the breathless old man. He dismounted, sat down beside his bicycle, and offered his panting father a cigarette. This was the most patent sign of his newly acquired power, his altered status, for up until then his father hadn't been supposed to know that he smoked, let alone that he possessed cigarettes. Bernd had broken a law, and the little white cylinder full of brown crumbs was his title to power. Wotan took the cigarette in silence, Bernd gave him a light, and the two of them smoked without exchanging a word.

An SS unit was stationed in Irmchen's village. The black uniforms and the shiny black boots in which the strapping young men strutted about had become the most striking feature of the village. "There are sixteen of them," said Irmchen. "A special detachment." She knew them all. She wore pale purple tunics and had somehow wangled a floor-length fur cape that made her look tall, slim, and beautiful. With her red hair and exotic dress, she cut as uncountrified a figure as the SS men. Bernd didn't know exactly what, but he sensed that something was going on. Irmchen seemed to belong to the unit; they were an occupying power.

Bernd's father seemed an outsider who had not

been initiated into the code, the system of signals. A visit to the village inn almost ended in a fight. The shiny black fighting cocks demanded music; ignoring the husband, they danced with Irmchen, invited themselves to her table with an air of ownership, and ordered for "our little lady" what they were evidently accustomed to ordering for her. They brought regards from Karl or Arnulf and reminisced about an evening spent together six days back. There was obviously an understanding between them and they were playing some sort of giddy game that Irmchen enjoyed and that humiliated her gray old goat of a husband. Abruptly he stood up and announced that they would have their dinner "at home." "Home" consisted of one room — there was another next door, but Irmchen's mother, the "Soup Chicken," was living in it. Unruffled, Irmchen set to work with her "magic touch." Working happily with odds and ends, she managed in no time to improvise an appetizer, a salad, and a soup. As nonchalantly as though gliding across the marketplace in her fur cape, she stood laughing over the hot plate in her apron. In pouring the wine, she infuriated Wotan by saying: "From the cellars of the SS, my dear." The atmosphere that evening, tense and at the same time jovial, made no sense to Bernd. One moment a serious quarrel seemed imminent, and in the next their affection for each other was unmistakable. Bernd couldn't have said why, but all this made him very tired, and he was soon drunk. Contemplating "the fat of the land," as Irmchen called it, he couldn't help wondering why his father should bring margarine and sausage from their own meager rations when Irmchen was so well supplied. Stuffing as much as possible into his mouth, he said to himself: All this really belongs to me. Afterward, he peed in the washbasin and without undressing fell asleep on the couch at the foot of the bed.

Later, through curtains of darkness, he heard panting, heaving, battle, as the two of them submerged each other in lust. Gurgling black water pulled Bernd down, washed away memory and perception; a whirlpool of surfeit, disgust, indifference, and drunkenness demolished his will to understand. Gone was his self-awareness.

On the way back, he had difficulty in hiding his loot, for of course he had taken as much as possible: a chunk of salami, half a bar of chocolate, a thick slice of bacon, and hardest of all to conceal, half a loaf of bread. This was his revenge for last night's misery: the bacon for the panting, the salami for the groaning and bucking. An anonymous cyclist, he left his father far behind him.

A few days later Bernd's father asked if he'd care to pick him up at the office that afternoon; they could do a bit of shopping. Bernd was quick to understand. This was his way of apologizing, for he loved his father's office, that whole remote world, the huge granite gray building on Dönhoffplatz, the bronze lions outside, the uniformed doorman in his little booth, who smiled benignly when Bernd said: "My father, Herr Direktor Walther, is expecting me." On his lucky days, he was allowed to go in alone, down the long corridors walled with brown slabs of majolica — a substance known to Bernd only in the form of cachepots for leafy plants. For Bernd the tracery, the swans, the lianas, and the water lilies with long, meticulously modeled roots were as good as a visit to the botanical gardens. The whole enormous building, with its hum of organized activity, its elevators with their impressive gates and bronze facings, their little velvet benches and mirrors, and another uniformed attendant who handled the lever affixed to the big round drum as easily as if he had never done anything else in all his life — on such days Bernd's ambition in life was to become an elevator boy — all this was more glorious than the toy department of any department store. True, when he went there before Christmas, it made him frantic with covetousness, but then, unattainable as all this was, there was a friendliness about it. After all, the giant teddy bears and fabulous motorcars were equally unattainable.

Moreover, these gigantic toys functioned; everybody played with them. The little carts, for instance, pushed down the corridors by still other uniformed attendants, stopping here and there to unload newspapers or pick up files. All this was the strange, dreamed-of grown-up world, it smelled like grown-ups and was as mysterious and out of reach as they were. His father's vestibule was a small room with green wallpaper and ribbed velvet curtains, one of which always seemed to be caught in a towering cactus. Here sat Fräulein Wilhelm, whom Bernd knew and liked, who wore incredibly short skirts, whom he had never seen without a cigarette, whose mahogany desk was marbled with cigarette burns, who made coffee while telephoning and seemed to do both uninterruptedly all day long. The tiny coffee machine and a tray with equally tiny square coffee cups were on a round marble-topped table, and beside them stood a photograph of the propaganda minister, inscribed in the lower left-hand corner: "For Gerlinde Wilhelm — Dr. Joseph Goebbels," and a vase, of the same rectilinear severity as the coffee set. In short, a mini-Chancellery, always decorated with fresh yellow flowers. Fräulein Wilhelm, who looked more like a Schad* painting than an Ufa poster, always had the same surprise ready for Bernd, a roll of licorice; he hated the brownish black stuff. Its bittersweet taste had become permanently associated with a visit to his father; it was like the three notes that preceded special announcements on the radio, the tune that introduced the newsreel at the movies. After that the curtain went up — the door to his father's room opened.

Friedrich-Wilhelm Walther was in a good mood

*Christian Schad (1894–1982), neorealist painter and inventor of a special graphic-photographic technique.

that day, affable, gracious. No "Bernd-Jörn," just a bemused "So there you are, you little rascal." He was always bemused in his office, moving things around on his desk, opening and closing drawers. Bernd had never quite fathomed that office; his intense curiosity about his father's retreat had never been satisfied — he needed time and leisure to incorporate a place into his system, to get the feel of the furnishings, the light, the colors, the smell.

There had never been time enough in his father's office. And today, as usual, Herr Walther slipped quickly into his gabardine topcoat, picked up his gloves — but not the briefcase that Bernd so passionately envied, which meant that they would be coming back here — and took an offhand leave of his secretary. "Good, good. So here we go. We're sure to find something for this young fellow. I have an idea that he needs a tracksuit." Bernd couldn't imagine why. He had a perfectly good tracksuit, and seeing there was no school and no sports, he didn't even need the one he had. But no matter, the shops and the big department stores would be fun. As long as they didn't end up with something made of Bleyle, that disgusting, extradurable knit good that took all the fun out of shopping. What he really wanted was a pair of shoes, because his low-cut sport shoes, fastened with buckles instead of laces, were too small and pretty well worn out. But he knew he didn't have enough clothing points left for shoes, even if there were any on the market. And his father was saving his points for the weekend presents he brought his guzzler of SS wine.

Nothing came of the expedition. They hadn't been on the street for more than ten minutes when the sirens started in. One of those frightful daylight raids by great squadrons of Flying Fortresses. Often whole neighborhoods collapsed, touched and condemned by the steel finger of vengeance. A sign directed father and son to the nearest shelter — air-raid shelters had been installed throughout the inner city, in ministries and apartment houses. This was ridiculous, Bernd thought — how often they had stood on the flat roof of their house, watching the silvery shimmering planes, watching their vapor trails and the white puffs of smoke as the flak shells burst. It wasn't at all unusual for well-dressed gentlemen and their fairy princesses to look down on the city in flames as they sipped their cocktails. "Oh God, how awful!" a lady would sigh while trying with a fingerful of saliva to stop the run she had made in her silk stocking while climbing through the narrow trapdoor to the roof. With the help of his company's construction gang, Herr Walther had installed an air-raid shelter in his own garden, a cozy, comfortable place, furnished with beds, woolen blankets, a thick carpet, a radio, a stove and a rudimentary bar, and stocked with food and candles. The public shelters were regarded as vulgar. In one of these public shelters, featuring stout wooden props, allegedly pressure-resistant steel doors, and an emergency exit encased in concrete, a nervous, frightened crowd had gathered. They glared at one another with suspicion and fear — fear of death from outside and fear of these people with whom they had been thrown together. Deep distrust inhibited conversation, admitting only of futile comments such as: "That was close," "That must have been a three-hundred-pounder," or "Oh my God, even down here you can hear the crackling of the fire." Twice the all clear was revoked by a new warning — a new wave of bombers was on its way. There was no radio in this shelter. When Bernd and his father left, it was dark outside — in the early afternoon.

The city was in flames. Great black smoke clouds hung low, traversed by the gray mortar dust from buildings that were still toppling. The air was rent by a sound composed of screams and moans, the cracking of gigantic housefronts, falling stone, and the hissing of fire. The raid was over, but the roaring inferno was just beginning, gathering strength from minute to minute.

Bernd is running. No matter where to. He can't breathe, his eyes are watering, his pulse is pounding in his ears. He runs into a street which at that same moment rears up like a great beast and falls back almost slowly with a hideous din. Great walls topple in an avalanche of dust. Suddenly the street becomes a chimney, with flames hissing through on both sides of him. My shoes, what's happening to my shoes, my hair, my eyes, air, there isn't any air, the flames are eating up all the air, a whirlwind of soot and ashes and heat, my shoes, weren't we going to buy shoes, no, a suit, my suit, my shoes are melting into the street, my suit is on fire, my hair, my eyebrows, no air to shout with, darkness.

When Bernd came to, he was sitting in a bar with his father. He had a big glass of schnapps in front of him. Hairless and shoeless, he was wrapped in a big blanket that smelled of fire. The heat had melted the asphalt in Friedrichstrasse, and his feet had got stuck in it. The flames from the houses to the right and left had shot upward, creating a draft; he had been unable to free himself from the airless heat. His hair, his eyebrows, his suit had burned to a crisp. And then an unknown woman had thrown a wet blanket over him and dragged him to a spot where the fire had gone out.

Father and son sat silent. Both drank schnapps as matter-of-factly as if that was their usual daily occupation.

Bernd thought nothing and felt nothing, not even pain. The schnapps offered a new, different kind of blackness. He didn't wake up until he felt something wet dripping on his scorched face. He was lying in bed beside his father, as though trying to crawl into him. Bernd smelled his hairbrush, a mixture of tallow and cognac. The Flying Fortresses had welded them together.

The Blueberry Orgy

"Coweyes looks like a scalded rat." These were the Snail's first words. A big Wehrmacht truck had ground to a halt in front of the house and she had jumped out. A battle was being fought over Görlitz and some soldiers had given her a lift, her last chance to escape. She arrived without luggage. Unruffled. As though returning from a day in the country.

Her return brought a quick change. The comradely cohabitation of father and son was thrown off balance. That was the end of their friendly slapdash suppers of fried potatoes and scrambled eggs. Their brief moment of fragile intimacy evaporated. They had never spoken of their black afternoon. Bernd told the Snail about the weekend visits, and she soon became his ally. Faced with a united front of his children, the father was infuriated by their inquisitorial questions about food coupons or cigarettes; oh, they knew where it all went. "He takes away the last crumb," said the Snail. "And we get a cup of grits for supper. I'm fed up." On most days, the two of them disappeared into Hermine's room as soon as their father came home in the evening. They lived together like strangers who had chanced to be assigned to the same house.

Startling news came over the radio. A counterattack had made a drastic change in the Silesian front. Görlitz, which could easily be reached by telephone, was out of danger and, wonder of wonders, the stores were selling their reserve stocks. Allegedly candles and soap, shoes and sweaters, milk powder and potatoes could be had without ration coupons. A paradise, less than a hundred and fifty miles southeast of gray, starving Berlin.

The Snail was quick to make up her mind. "We'll go to Görlitz. Think of it, Coweyes, we'll get everything we need, we won't even ask the old man, and we won't give him anything. Let his SS moll feed him. We'll take Ani with us, she'll be a help." Ani was her girlfriend Anette, who lived with her divorced mother in Kreuzberg. She was indeed a help. She was able to borrow a bit of money, and she was pretty — a priceless asset in a train crowded with soldiers.

The Görlitz station in Berlin had been badly bombed and was closed to civilians. Still, the three of them managed to get through with their big suitcases and knapsacks by playing the part of frightened children looking for their parents. The flood of frantic refugees, soldiers, *Volkssturm* men, and nurses made any effective check impossible. Without tickets — for none were being sold — the three ragged, hungry-looking children smuggled themselves into an eastbound train. They took turns standing guard in the corridor. When Bernd saw a group of military policemen checking the compartments, he sent the girls to the toilet. "My big sister has our tickets," he explained. When the big sister failed to appear, the MPs got suspicious and pounded on the door. The two girls had seen enough movies. "My friend is sick," Ani shouted. "She's in terrible pain, I think she's going to faint." Ani opened the door and dragged the Snail out. The soldiers were only too glad to help the two young things. The Snail was so frightened she began to cry in earnest. In the end they were all together in the compartment reserved for the military police. There they were safe. They told the soldiers a touching story, explaining why they had to go to Görlitz and whom they were going to see there. Sipping ersatz coffee out of tin cups, they dreamed of jam and salami. The three young men with the striped semicircular badges were delighted with the company of the inventive young girls.

In Görlitz the station was closed. Only military personnel with valid papers were allowed to leave the building. The city had been declared a prohibited

THE BLUEBERRY ORGY

zone. The platforms, stairways, over- and underpasses were crowded with civilians — refugees from Silesia but also from Görlitz itself — pushing and shoving or just sitting there with their bundles. No one knew when another train would be leaving or, if there was one, where it would be going to. The train they had come on showed no sign of ever going anywhere, but already a howling mob was taking it by storm. Better an immobilized lifeboat than the raging sea.

"Kids, I've got an idea — follow me quick, but don't run, that would attract attention. Just try and look as if we wanted to get back into the train." Bernd speaking. "Way at the end of the platform there's a freight elevator. I know, because when we were called out of school to help with the refugee trains, we used that elevator for the big milk cans full of coffee substitute. The elevator isn't working. But next to it there's an iron staircase that leads into a tunnel that surfaces outside the station. If we can just get the manhole open." Coweyes was proud of himself. It wasn't those flirtatious liars with their tears and fainting fits that could save this situation, it was him. They had wangled a few half-cups of coffee with ersatz cream — but he knew the way to the soap and salami. The manhole cover stuck and squeaked and groaned, but in the end it gave way to their combined efforts and the three hungry cats emerged in the station square. Here they were in the Promised Land. They crept through deserted streets in darkness relieved only by an occasional fillet of light from the headlight slits of a blacked-out military vehicle. The Snail still had the keys to the apartment belonging to Else, her old governess, where she had been living when "rescued" by the truck convoy. The building was empty, dark, and cold. All the windows had been smashed — by thieves, by bombs? The apartment was miraculously intact. Telephone, radio, light, stove — unexpectedly, absurdly, everything functioned. Light-headed with relief at arriving safely, they set out in search of Cockaigne. That was what they had come for.

They broke into the basement and found potatoes and jars of blueberry preserves. That's all there was. The girls made blueberry soup with potato dumplings, and when the light went out — power cut or Russian bombardment? — they sat on Else's double bed, shivering in the flickering candlelight, dipping sticky, crumbling potato dumplings into a big enamel bowl full of blueberry preserve. The juice ran down over their chins and hands, stained the sheets and quilts. In gorging themselves, they appeased their hunger and banished their fear.

In the defeated city everything was for sale, but there were no customers. Most of the inhabitants had fled from the approaching Red Army and were not there to buy the treasures the shops had been hiding for years and now suddenly offered for sale, things for which people no longer had any ration coupons left: candles and soap, lard and noodles, sugar, rice, even coffee and chocolate. You couldn't find everything where you might have expected, but in the shoe store they knew where stockings were available, and the old lady in the knit-goods store could direct you to a source of honey. As though to unburden themselves of their guilt, the shopkeepers opened their storerooms, and, before long, stocks of potatoes, canned milk, mittens, and castor oil were heaped up in the blueberry heaven.

The return trip was easier to manage. The role of poor lost children going back to their parents in Berlin presented no difficulties. There was no need of money. What little the children had had been spent. Refugees were no more obliged to pay for transportation than were soldiers heading for the front. Their unwieldy baggage aroused no suspicion; naturally refugees would be trying to save their last remaining possessions. And now the salami and packages of Mondamin were no longer rattling around in their minds, but safe in the baggage racks overhead. In the Berlin station there were always plenty of ragged, half-starved *Ostarbeiter*,* who were penned up in bleak dormitories at night but allowed to move about freely during the day. Realizing that they would not be able to manage their suitcases and car-

*Literally, "Eastworkers," for the most part Russians or Poles, who because of the acute labor shortage had been brought in to do heavy or menial jobs for negligible wages.

tons and knapsacks unaided in the S-Bahn (elevated railway), the travelers hired two of them, promising to pay them in potatoes. Arrived at Ani's mother's place in Kreuzberg, the young people were obliged to unpack their treasures before the covetous eyes of their porters. They sensed the danger. Obviously, these *Ostarbeiter* were half maddened by hunger. Thus far the young people had been engaged in what they regarded as an amusingly adventurous test of courage; they had played Indians; blueberry soup had been their war paint. But now they were afraid. Knowing that these men had sunk to the bottom-most depths of human degradation and were capable of anything, they reacted quickly and wisely. Like wood lice, which save themselves by abandoning a good part of their prey, they sacrificed a whole carton of potatoes. True, it was only one of three, but the porters were so overwhelmed by such unexpected generosity that they hurried away, thinking there must have been some mistake.

It was Christmas in the little apartment. Cans and candles and woolens and paper bags were piled up and Ani's mother took mouthfuls of everything at once. Then she had a splendid idea. She would make potato pancakes and applesauce. Exhausted by fear and excitement and strain, light-headed with relief, the children had only one thought: to celebrate. "And we won't give the old man anything," said the Snail. "Not a thing. Let him take delicacies to his SS moll. He won't get any from us. We'll just stay here. He doesn't know we're back. We'll live like kings."

A few hours later the kings were suffering from cramps. They had fried the potato pancakes in the only fat they had found — castor oil. From then on brother and sister referred to this ailment as "Görlitz's revenge."

The Russians Came All in White

"The Americans, Papa, the Amis, Papa, the Amis are here!" A cry of joy. Nothing more to be afraid of. Coweyes raced through the cellar until he found his father and pulled him to one of the barred windows. In the leaden gray morning light bowed khaki figures were darting forward, clutching tommy guns as though for support. Shots could be heard, but from far away. Herr Walther looked old and spent with his three-day beard. "My God, the Americans!" he gasped. It sounded almost like a prayer of thanksgiving. And then: "Ilse, make us a pot of coffee."

The Walther family was living in what was left of the house. That was the cellar — which was underground only on the street side; on the side of the sloping garden, it was on a level with the ground. The cellar door opened out on what had been the terrace. The rest of the house was a thing of the past. Only a few days before, at the beginning of May, aerial mines dropped by "sewing machines," as the still-arrogant Berliners contemptuously called the Russian monomotored planes, had devastated the whole street.

The warning system was out of commission, and they had all spent the night in the house rather than in the garden shelter or the big concrete bunker where the major general had rented a room: the Snail, who accordingly had not packed her stylish leather overnight bag containing such absolute necessities as powder, lipstick, mirror, a few perfumed, cork-tipped cigarettes, a pair of stockings with black seams, and a picture of René; Bernd, who in his black HY knapsack had hidden air-raid candles, a can of Biomalt, burn bandages, and, his holy of holies, a can of airman's chocolate; Wotan, his briefcase bulging with important papers; and "the Sparrow," with a torn midwife's satchel. The Sparrow was the major general's unmarried sister from Stettin, who had fled from the Russians. She had been running the household for the last four months and was cordially detested by the Snail and Cow-eyes. They had never had any use for "my dear sister Ilse" or her hideous old-fashioned apartment, where they regularly spent a day in the course of their summer trips to the Baltic and were regaled with sticky rose-hip liqueur, sticky dumplings, and sticky stewed apricots. Her apartment seemed to consist exclusively of an endless corridor, great squeaky cupboards, and countless gigantic beds. The Sparrow was tiny; she had shriveled purple cheeks and a wee little bun, and she invariably wore a dark silk blouse with a cameo pinned to it, "to show which is the front," as Hermine put it. The pastor's spinster daughter idolized her brother; early hatred had turned to tortured love; for in his younger days the future major general and bank president had taken as much as he could from the Pomeranian parsonage; as a cadet and young lieutenant, he had lived in luxury, expecting his father to pay his gambling debts and defray the cost of his horse and groom. After that the impoverished parsonage couldn't afford to give his daughter an education. She was left "on the shelf," in the fullest sense of the word. And since everything about her was small, her heart and brain were without capacity for revenge. When she spoke of her "dear brother," she meant it; and she felt the same doglike love for his children, who detested her.

They had always made fun of her "monkey coat," a shaggy brown fur garment that she wore summer and winter, and her "skating boots," meaning her ankle-high laced shoes that looked as if they had never been young. A certain plaintive tone in which she called the children to dinner had earned her the nickname "Sparrow," and their feeling for their father's "dear sister" Ilse was no more than what they might have felt for an absurd piece of furniture, a squeaky tea trolley, for instance. "Damned if it isn't the Sparrow," was all they could think of saying when she arrived from Stettin with all her remaining belongings in one suitcase. "She wasn't really in any danger. Even the Russians wouldn't have touched her." They could only laugh at her grief over the "old rags" she had lost. "She should be glad she's rid of the stuff."

But now the Walthers were rid of their own "stuff." All were awakened by deafening noise, collapsing walls, crashing glass, explosions, hissing fire, screams. Exploding bombs had plowed up the garden and blasted the *Yuricke* like a hurricane. Gone were windows, doors, and internal walls. The house groaned and sagged, but it was still there.

Bernd reacted mechanically, as though drilled. He had been through this too often, he was only too familiar with bursting bombs, burning houses, and screaming people. The special smell of crumbling mortar and splintered wood was well known to him. In his room everything had collapsed, his bed was half covered with wreckage, but he himself was unharmed. He quickly put on his tracksuit, which lay on the floor within easy reach, and grabbed his flashlight and knapsack. Where was his sister? That was his first thought. She was his only friend. And if anything had happened to her, he was to blame.

This René, whose picture she kept in her little bag, this René with his ridiculous actor's mustache and pomaded hair, actually existed. The Snail had planned to elope with him this very night. A foolish, adventurous plan. "I want to get out of here. I can't bear the sight of the old man anymore. I can't listen to his idiotic final-victory crap anymore. I'm clearing out. René will get me forged papers, he's French, after all. We'll go somewhere in the West. Don't worry, Coweyes, I'll manage somehow, somewhere. Maybe we'll go to our French relatives. Then I'll come and get you. I'm not spending another day in the clutches of that idiotic Wotan." Bernd was her confidant; she had sent him yesterday to deliver the decisive letter. But the streets were littered with glass and shell fragments; both his bicycle tires had been punctured; after two hours of pushing he had given up and come home. The U-Bahn (subway) and S-Bahn had both stopped running. Hermine's elopement had come to nothing. And he was to blame.

The stairwell had caved in. There was no way of getting to his sister's room. Outside his room there was only a gaping hole with the ground floor at the bottom of it. The corridor leading to the Snail's room wasn't there anymore. Through the holes that had once been windows he could see flickering flames, whether from inside or outside the house he had no way of knowing. From time to time an explosion broke the strange, uncanny silence. There was no human sound. Like a skeletal finger Bernd's flashlight with the compulsory blackout slit groped its way across the hole to Hermine's room, revealing clouds of plaster dust, nothing else. Not a sound.

Then suddenly Wotan, hitherto anesthetized by fear, woke up, screaming. "My pistol! Where's my pistol? My pistol is gone! I can't find my pistol!" Bernd wasn't interested in his father's pistol. But the screams reminded him that his father's room was next to his own and that his sister's lay beyond it. It hadn't occurred to him that with the partitions removed one could float through the house as in a dream, without regard for doors or hallways. Cautiously, he groped his way past overturned cupboards, over beams and vestiges of walls. The partition between his father's room and his sister's room had collapsed, and so had cupboards that had stood against it. It had fallen on his sister's bed and the ceiling had fallen on top of it. The Snail was buried.

The left sleeve of Bernd's tracksuit was white with plaster, his nose was running, and he was screaming inaudibly. Water ran out of him as from a burst water pipe. The Snail was dead and he was to blame. Why hadn't he ridden to René's on his rims? Why hadn't he tried to mend his tires? Why hadn't he walked off with someone else's bicycle? Why hadn't he stopped some military vehicle and asked for a lift? In those days soldiers were always picking up children and even giving them bread. In the distance he heard the old man's idiotic screaming about his pistol; he had found a way down to the ground floor. Bernd heard what was left of the stairway cracking, collapsing piece by piece under the weight of his father, who for some reason or other was trying to come up again.

Minutes had passed since the raid. Somewhere ack-ack guns were barking. Searchlights swept the sky. With the help of their light, Bernd shoveled and tugged and fought his way through a tangle of beams and rods and wires, a bleeding, squeaking, panting rat. "She's alive! Don't let her be dead, I'll get her out, she promised to send for me, I'll go to René's tomorrow, I'll give her my airman's chocolate and my knitted Norwegian sock slippers. Snail, dear Snail, don't be dead, oh, please be alive." His thoughts raced ahead of his bleeding hands. Water flowed from his eyes, mouth, and nose, and into his trousers as well.

Suddenly he saw blood. A searchlight beam shone through, showing him that the wall and the cupboard had fallen obliquely over the bed, leaving an empty space, and that the mountain of rubble hadn't tumbled until after that. The Snail was wedged in. She was unconscious and bleeding, but she was not buried. And she was not dead.

It was still fairly early when the Walther family gathered in what had been the garden. The major general was speechless; he had indeed been out of his mind for a few minutes; the Sparrow was daubing and fussing over Hermine's bleeding head wound. Hermine looked comically tragic in her tattered muslin nightgown. She was furious, it was all her brother's fault, and she was making him suffer for it. He implored her to let him feed her. "Come on, it's *my* Biomalt I'm giving you, it's the last can, we mustn't let the old man see it. I'll give you my airman's chocolate, too."

Three houses farther on the fire was still raging. The *Yuricke* was not on fire, but the Haunschilds' beautiful house was one blazing torch. Bernd knew the house well; it was the finest house in the neighborhood. Haunschild had been the sole owner of a brewery since 1936 when Herr Jakob, his partner, had been forced out. The Haunschilds had a pretty daughter, and the families had been friends until Herr Walther married. Now Frau Haunschild was dancing about in the wreckage, howling the same words over and over: "All gone! All gone! All gone!" A dim white ghost dancing around her collapsing home. "All gone! All gone!" There was a note of senseless triumph in her cries. Hermine began to laugh. "My God, Coweyes, listen to the old cow, crying about her junk. I can't bear it. Really, Coweyes, we mustn't quarrel anymore, we mustn't be like that, making such a fuss over a lot of junk. It's sickening."

Hermine felt profound contempt for possessions, the contempt of one who had always had everything and took it for granted that one owned a house. How such things are acquired she had no idea. One just had them. She thought herself ever so worldly-wise, but her experience was very limited. One of her maxims was: "A house with a street lamp in front of it is better than one without a street lamp in front of it." And another: "A street that's called avenue or boulevard or lane is better than one that's just called street."

Such remarks as well as her contempt for possessions had made a profound impression on Bernd. He admired the same attitude in his stepmother, and suddenly remembered two entirely different episodes. Shortly before Irmchen's appearance on the scene, Frau Haunschild's daughter had once asked him over for cocoa. That same afternoon a handsome young officer arrived to collect her new BMW cabriolet with red leather seats, which had been requisitioned for the Wehrmacht. Frau Haunschild was standing behind the curtain of the bay window. Bernd had always thought her big potted azaleas much more impressive than the poor little cyclamens in white pots at home. Frau Haunschild had stood there sobbing: a high, thin sound like the squeaking of a mouse.

Soon someone had come for Irmfried Walther's dark green Horch with the unwarranted coronet. Her eyes had narrowed with rage, but then she had snapped her fingers and said: "Oh, well, who needs a car! I just feel sorry for the young fellow." To her, property was always desirable and desired, but one was never really entitled to it, it was more like loot or theft. Life was a poker game — you could win and you could lose. Irmfried Im Felden was not bourgeois. Much as they hated her, both children came to recognize that.

Then those two wicked dwarfs stood torn and bleeding, yet grinning as their home burned; beside them the pistol-mad Wotan and the wet Sparrow, behind them the groaning and crumbling and crackling of the sinking *Yuricke,* and before their eyes the Haunschilds' blazing torch with the property-crazed dervish woman dancing around it. Tongues of flame transformed her fluttering white nightgown into an orange-colored evening dress dotted with green, made her singed hair glitter and, amid the flaring and fading of searchlight beams and the sadly diminished popping of the antiaircraft guns, transformed her hand-wringing funeral march into a dance step. This was the last dance. Next morning the Russians were there.

Bernd's Amis were not Americans, they were Russians. He had never seen an American or an American uniform, he only knew that they wore khaki uniforms and that their steel helmets were flatter than the German ones. Russians, on the other hand, were beyond imagining; Russians were chaos, death, the end of the world. And Americans were nothing of the kind. The family had been waiting eagerly for the Americans; for weeks they had been listening to American broadcasts over Hermine's tiny ivory-colored radio and heard that they were not too far from Berlin. The night had been an inferno. Bernd and Hermine had dug and searched through the wreckage and helped the neighbors. Then long after midnight they had fallen asleep on cots in the cellar, while the *Yuricke* smoked and crackled and crashed overhead.

Bernd's "the Americans, Papa, the Amis" woke everyone up. At first nothing happened. The strange soldiers had groped their way forward as far as Bernd's school, which had been converted into a hospital and was being defended by a handful of trigger-happy SS men. In the gray of dawn, the Walthers crept up the intact cellar stairs to survey the wreckage. Their first impression was that apart from the outer walls nothing was left — only wreckage, fragmented furniture, tatters of masonry. They had never realized that walls had wires running through them. They saw radiators dangling from pipes; the upstairs bathroom seemed intact, but the stairway leading to the second floor was gone. Wotan had demolished the last steps while looking for his Mauser.

The Russians came all in white.

In the afternoon of that hot day in May — the Walther family had pulled and tugged, cleared rubble, disengaged two ground-floor windows, and barricaded others with remnants of shutters — a crowd of boisterous, shouting, and singing nuns appeared and settled down in the churned-up garden. The enormous white coifs of the Ursuline sisters from the Catholic hospital could be seen bobbing up and down behind a camel at the far end of the garden — bedouins on Richthofenstrasse. In flowing robes, gray and white, skirt over skirt, their long capes outspread like bats' wings, flocks of chattering, chirping nun-birds sailed down the ravaged slope, led by the gravely striding camel, which stopped now and then to chomp a sprig of lilac or laburnum on its way.

Bernd was first to venture out of the house. The nuns were slapping their thighs and hugging one another. They had made a fire: a big iron pot hung over it, and a few brawny nuns were bringing up enormous milk cans.

The nuns were Russian soldiers. They had broken into the clothes cupboards at the Saint Augustine Hospital. They had never seen such costumes and in their drunken euphoria they put on the starched coifs, threw the capes over their uniforms, and fastened various other articles of female attire to their uniforms. Black mustaches and unshaven faces could be seen under butterfly coifs; rosaries clinked against ammunition belts; amulets dangled between the red star and the hammer and sickle: Bernd couldn't take his eyes off them. The bearded nuns plunged ladles into the milk cans, drank, and let the kneeling camel drink out of them. An Asian-looking sister with a black mustache and flowing skirts tossed something to Bernd, and Bernd ran zigzagging like a rabbit into the house. "Throw that away this minute," his father bellowed. "It's poisoned, they'll kill us all, my God, these hordes, these murderers, these subhumans. Is nothing to be spared us? Oh, the disgrace! Chocolate cookies all ready to poison us with, I knew it all along. But I can speak Russian, I learned it in 1916, in the Crimea — Ilse, make a pot of coffee, I'm going to welcome the victors — oh God, so that's what we lost the war to!"

Bernd got there first. An irresistible force drew him to the camp fire. He had hopes of more good things that his father wouldn't be able to take away from him. The nuns welcomed him; they poked around in the big iron pot and gave him big fat chunks of meat with some kind of grits sticking to them. Bernd forgot about poison and bolted the meat, his first in weeks. Suddenly the smell came to him: the milk cans were full of wine. After the first ladleful he threw up, to the delight of the bearded nuns, who kept singing the same foreign song, laughing, and smacking the camel. Then they started bellowing "Hitleh kaputt," and pissing in great vaulted streams from under their starched skirts. Bernd saw his father coming with the coffeepot and scented danger in the sudden silence — those soldiers weren't used to hearing a German speak Russian. One of them took Herr Walther's watch, ever so gently, just as a moment before he had pushed aside Bernd's sweaty, shoulder-length, reddish brown hair. The Russians drank coffee from the spout of the coffeepot and gave the major general a ladleful of wine. The camel sagged to its knees.

In the cool of the evening the family sat in the

former laundry room on an old garden bench that was leaning against the huge ancient mangle. They were too tired to do or even to think anything much. Actually, there was nothing to do. The flames of the Haunschild house had barely died away. The victors around their camp fires were growing noisier by the minute. They were beginning to look around. The neighborhood women had hidden in the garden shelter, which could still be crawled into. Not Hermine. "You're crazy if you think you can coop me up," she said to her father. "I'm going to lie down upstairs. What did we dig up a couch for?" Bernd dozed off on his bench while Wotan and the Sparrow exchanged whispers.

Bernd was awakened by shots and shouts and general pandemonium. The bearded nuns were swarming through the night, brandishing their pistols, shooting into windows. Now they were wearing their holsters over their skirts, and their cartridge belts were slung crosswise over their shoulders, crushing their stiff white blouses. They had discovered the women in the shelter and were dragging them out like so many milk cans.

Wotan's servile self-importance of the afternoon brought ten or twelve of the Russians into the house. One had nothing on under his white skirt; another was wearing only trousers and a crumpled white coif; the friendly Asian, stark naked under a flowing cape, was shooting off his tommy gun at random. The Sparrow sat whimpering on the mangle, clutching the cast-iron lever like a weapon. A soldier was patting her in a counterproductive attempt to soothe her. Frau Haunschild sat huddled under an old garden table, sobbing so loudly that the Russians soon dragged her out of her hiding place. "It's all your fault, Herr Walther," she screamed. "Yours and nobody else's. They're going to kill us all, and all because of you." The major general, whose pathetic scraps of Russian only amused the drunken soldiers, was being tossed from one to another like a ball. Through a multicolored mist Bernd saw him rise and fall. The friendly Asian had sat Bernd down on his lap and was stroking his long hair. From time to time he ordered a ladleful of soup for him. Bernd was only dimly aware of what was going on. He was sitting in a whirring Ferris wheel, clutching something, the hair on the soldier's chest or perhaps his tommy gun, which was as hot as the soldier's dark skin. One moment his head was reeling with dizziness, the next he was keenly alert. Through a rent in the fog of noise and sweetish salty-fishy stench he would suddenly see nuns' coifs sailing about and church candles brandished like sabers. He reveled in the horror of it. The ground was sinking from under his feet. More and more of the soldiers had thrown off their boots and trousers. Mud-spattered, their torn white gowns spotted with blood, the soldiers would impale a coif or hang amulets, rosaries, crosses, and holy pictures on their erect members. Two were punching each other mercilessly because one had set fire to the other's pubic hair with his candle. Bernd's Asian was feeling him up, his eyes had narrowed to slits. Then suddenly he struck Bernd on the behind with his tommy gun and screamed with a raucous laugh: "You nix woman, *yob tvoyu mat*, you nix woman!"

Bernd fled in terror, threw himself down, and crawled on all fours to the furnace room. Trembling, bleeding, covered with sweat and vomit, he burrowed into the pile of coke.

Someone pulled him out and dragged him back. The old mangle had caught fire; the heavy worm-eaten wood was smoldering; the Sparrow sat beside it whimpering, a martyred witch. A drenched soldier rubbed the coal off Bernd's face and hands with wine. The cellar was empty, but the house was full of noise. Bernd was as wide awake as a rabid dog. He wanted to live. He bit and scratched as they dragged him up the cellar stairs.

The soldiers had discovered that there were more rooms on the ground floor. A few had climbed in through the windows, and their comrades in the cellar had heard them. A shorn Russian with a priest's soutane thrown over his shoulders but otherwise naked was standing at the sagging piano. Holding a long, flickering candle in one hand, he was trying to play the piano with his penis. Striking always the same notes, he kept roaring: "Hitleh kaputt, Hitleh kaputt!" Someone had defecated in the open piano, and the hammer squooshed on the last note.

The clerico-phallic piano player was so drunk he could hardly stand, but that didn't prevent another soldier, who had torn a telephone from its moorings, from holding it up to his mouth. Into it the Red Army pianist bellowed his "Hitleh kaputt, kaputt, kaputt."

Hermine was somewhere at the back of the room. Bernd was too dizzy and sick and terrified to know, or want to know, more. The soldier forced him to eat, and when he turned his head, he saw, only two or three feet away from him, his father kneeling in the dingy candlelight. Bare to the waist, on his head a coif, in his mouth a pistol, and on his hairy chest the Soviet star hanging from a chain. He was sopping wet. Bernd knew beyond any possible doubt: They're going to shoot him. The time dragged on, the pistol was not fired. The bald-headed penis-pastor collapsed right next to the major general, who was saved by the tumultuous applause. The naked pianist tore the coif off Herr Walther's head and hung it on his own penis. Bernd's father tried to crawl into the dark corner where his sister was being executed. Suddenly the "Hitleh-kaputt" singer was beside him. Now only one shoulder was covered by the black soutane, the white, bloodstained bands were bobbing up and down beside his still-erect member. Once again he thrust his pistol into the major general's mouth. A shot, a whimper. That must be his father's death. Bernd didn't look up. He lay in slippery wetness, in feces, blood, wine, and urine. The smell cut into him, aroused him, made him strangely alert, as though suspended in midair. He rolled under the slanting piano. Through the lyre formed by the pedals he saw the bald-naked-phallic-piano-playing priest thrusting and rethrusting his member into a nun's coif. Behind a cloud of white fluff he was brandishing a pistol; and under the huge butterfly with its great fluttering wings a chain with a red Soviet star on it swung back and forth, back and forth over a bare, matted gray chest.

The *Yuricke* Hoists Blood Red Sails

The Snail cleared out. The witches' sabbaths of the Russians had gone on night after night. The school at the far corner of the garden was now a Russian barracks. Nightly, the Russians carried out the recommendations of a leaflet:

> Kill, kill. There is no such thing as an innocent German, whether living or unborn! Carry out Comrade Stalin's program: exterminate the fascist beast in his burrow. Humble the racial arrogance of Germanic women, take them by force. Take them as your rightful booty. Brave, victorious soldiers of the Red Army: Kill!

Wotan's lamentations about the hordes were repugnant, but so were the hordes. "Coweyes, you gotta help me, I'm getting out of here. Try and get in touch with René — we'll get through somehow, no matter where to. We'll go to France." She herself was unable to go out. A girl in those days couldn't show herself on the street.

Hitler was dead, the war was over — the people knew it, but it left them cold. Nothing mattered; all they wanted was to eat and be left alone. For a while, if you could find a telephone that was still working, you might get a kick out of calling friends in the western suburbs, only a few S-Bahn stations away, who were still living in Nazi Germany. But not for long. Nazi Germany soon ceased to exist. Even Wotan's pistol was gone; to the general indignation he had thrown it into the concrete reservoir at the end of the garden. He had done it secretly while drawing water. Then three corpses had been sighted at the bottom of the reservoir — and that was the water people used for making coffee. Wotan had grown very quiet. He had stopped asking questions. Where was Bernd keeping himself, how had he come by a bag of flour, why were his trouser pockets full of semolina? One day Bernd went with the Haunschilds to a bombed-out brewery at the other end of the city. Where the workers had supposedly slaughtered a dray horse with hammers, knives, and a big saw. Bernd brought home a big piece of hide with scraps of meat sticking to it. It was like a bloody piece of the brown pony-skin coat out of his mother's wardrobe, only the big buttons were missing. That same day he had managed to reach René. While the Sparrow was making sauerbraten out of

THE SURVIVOR

the pony skin in the washtub, he whispered the good news to his sister: "Man, we're cooking with gas. René is living in a DP camp, and he's got some kind of papers. There's a German bomber pilot with him, a young kid, escaped from an English prison camp, stole some papers somewhere, and speaks English perfectly. They're pulling out Monday."

For the two of them the sauerbraten from the brewery was a sad farewell dish. Bernd's parting gift to his sister consisted of a stolen pushcart, a woolen blanket, and two cans of potted eel. "Coweyes," she said. "You gotta help me, I gotta write the old man a letter. I can't do it. You were always good at composition — write it for me, something about good-bye and fed up and France. Any old thing."

Bernd had to carry various messages back and forth. And then one afternoon at the end of May, while his father was poking around in the compost heap under the gnarled walnut tree, Bernd wrote the letter. That night he helped his sister climb out of the ground-floor window, fastened the shutters from inside, and lay down on his cot in the laundry room.

When he woke up in the morning, his father was standing there. Bernd had never seen him in such a state; he was wearing his gray-and-red-striped terry-cloth bathrobe, which he had rescued from the ruins; it always smelled slightly of hair, cognac, and shaving cream. His "cactus legs," as his wife contemptuously called them, were planted in old bedroom slippers. In one hand he held a tiny bunch of primulas and a thin ring with a jewel in it, in the other a sheet of paper torn out of a school copybook, covered with Hermine's scribble: the letter.

The retired major general was unable to speak; he was crying, a wrinkled old child with thin hair, shattered beyond all shame. "Read this, Bernd — it's from Hermine. She's gone. Gone away. On her eighteenth birthday."

Sitting on the wobbly cot, Bernd shook his long, reddish brown hair out of his face and pretended to be surprised. "What? Gone? Where to?" And then with evident emotion he read his own letter. "Dear Papa, I can't stand it here anymore, the Russians and all the scenes and fights. I've been wanting to go for a long time, I couldn't find a way, but now I have a chance. I'm going to Paris with a displaced Frenchman, we'll stay with Uncle Gedat. You'll be better off without me in the house. Hermine."

Bernd now thought the letter unnecessarily cruel. The style appealed to his vanity but he was ashamed of his pretense. For the first time in his life he felt sorry for his father. Since that afternoon in the air-raid shelter his feelings toward his father had somehow softened. Now he wished Hermine hadn't omitted his "Take care of yourself. Your daughter, Hermine." And most of all he wished that in the excitement they hadn't both forgotten the birthday. His sobbing father, holding the primulas and his dead wife's ring, which he had shoveled out of the dung, looked just too pathetic. The sauerbraten repeated on Bernd. "Oh, well," he heard himself say, "she won't get very far. René may be French, but she isn't." He had said too much, but his father was too excited to understand about René. Just then the Sparrow was making coffee. Bernd took a Russian cigarette he had swiped and set it down beside his father's cup.

The old man was dying. He spent a whole year dying. An officer without any army, cornered, with nobody, not even himself, to whom he could give orders. Powerless to attack, to defend, or even to surrender and raise the white flag. The meaning had gone out of his life; his humiliations, like maggots and beetles, had eaten away his roots. He simply stopped living. Like an animal sensing that death is near, he dug a burrow for himself and his brood.

The *Yuricke* was patched up. One by one roofing tiles were taken from the orphaned houses nearby. The old man proved to be an able builder; for the first time he taught Bernd something and talked to him during periods that grew longer and longer, told him how he had learned these skills in 1916, while a prisoner in Russia. The two of them would be squatting on the flat roof. Now and then Bernd would sacrifice a Russian cigarette with a long cardboard mouthpiece or roll one from army newspaper and *machorka* tobacco. With the help of wires and broken pipes, they would piece tatters of wall together and cover them with scraps of carpets and blankets. For the windows Bernd found something ideal in a doctor's office: some squares of red plastic X-ray films. It could easily be cut and fitted into the windows. Lungs, stomachs, and intestines were discernible when the sun shone on these wavy, barely translucent panes. The whole house was bathed in a reddish violet* light that cast anatomical squiggles on the walls and floors. The *Yuricke* had hoisted bloody sails adorned with human entrails.

More and more often the old man spat blood. When his room was more or less ready, he lay down in the cracked, wobbly old bed and never got up again. Fever and his rotting lungs kept him bathed in a cloud of sweat, sputum, and fear; bit by bit, his bony energy crumbled away. Nothing was left but occasional grumbling. He made his son sleep in his room. Often Bernd retched with disgust when his father's cadaverous yellow hand clutched bloody rags after an agonizing coughing fit, when he dragged the urinal with the phosphorescent rim from under the bed, when his feeble rales went on and on. Bernd rolled up into a ball, on the defensive. He felt no pity. This helpless dwindling repelled him. The blood-spitting skeleton with the gray beard full of foaming spittle and the steadily expanding eyes, who spoke Russian in his sleep, who on waking told him the story of *The Forgotten Village*,† who breathed hot foulness into his face over the chess-

---

*The X-ray film of those days turned reddish brown with age.
†By Theodor Kröger.

board, who was perpetually begging for medicine or food, gave him the shudders.

Here Bernd saw his chance and took it. He bought his freedom from the sickroom where the retired major general was coughing his life away beside reddish violet X rays of human pancreases and spinal cords. The black market offered him freedom.

Life had gone back to normal. The law of the market, the rules of supply and demand, were in force again. The steppes had given way to Texas. The Americans had occupied parts of the city: gum-chewing athletic victors, smelling of antiseptic soap, negligently letting one foot dangle over the side of their jeeps. A smiling new army of occupation, vigorous, cheerful, bountiful. Once again everything had its price, its equivalent — a bosom, an orange, a piece of ass, a chocolate bar. Bernd admired everything, the clean uniforms, the jeeps, the throaty, easygoing way of talking, the casual, contemptuous way in which these soldiers flicked honey-fragrant cigarettes at the feet of the avidly waiting vanquished. White wine from milk cans had given way to Nescafé, chunks of meat sticky with millet gruel to Hershey bars; and while the Russian had gone a-courting with a pistol, the newcomer's weapon was a pair of nylon stockings. It didn't take Bernd long to catch on. Like a pack rat he carried various household articles to his old school building — the eagle at the entrance now carried the Stars and

Stripes in its talons instead of the gallows cross.*
The Amis had turned the school yard into a bazaar.
Bernd knew the building like the back of his hand.
He soon found out when the soldiers had roll call,
when they were in the mess hall, and when they
were off duty. Thus, he had no difficulty in stealing
fountain pens, flashlights, and cigarettes, which it
was easy to trade for something else a few streets
further on. In next to no time he had picked up the
elements of the language, first the numbers, then
the essential phrases. He soon stopped asking: "How
much late is it?" His life had become an equation.
Two hours of freedom from the blood-spitting ghost
= 1 HY dagger = 100 Camels = 1 pound of cocoa
and 1 can of corned beef.

With mixed feelings of contempt and breadwinner's pride he brought home what he had acquired by theft, barter, or skulduggery. His feelings had become thought and he thought in terms of price schedules — this was the price of his freedom, and here he did not cheat. His stomach tightened with pleasure when he saw his father's greedy fingers baffled by the unfamiliar packaging, by the boxes of cookies or the tins of ham larded with raisins that you opened by pulling a metal ring. Bernd would sit in a chair as far as possible from the bed, taking in the picture: the awkward fingering and then the

*The hooked cross, or swastika, of the Nazi flag.

smacking, slavering lips when the Sparrow served up scrambled eggs made from the egg powder, the plate held against the sweaty pajamas, the lips that had grown thinner than ever in a face of skin and bone, the horny, yellowish toenails sticking out from under the soiled gray quilt.

Salvation came from the black soldiers and from Menne. Manfred Degen had been Bernd's best friend in school before the whole class was shipped off to the country. He had sometimes bested Bernd in German composition and at handball always. He was at the head of the class, but intelligent. They had always competed, but without hard feelings: two firms manufacturing the same article. Now Bernd ran into him while rummaging, as he often did, through the ruins of a big apartment house, on the lookout for something that might be used, sold, or exchanged. He often unearthed treasure, an alarm clock, a radio, once even a pair of ski boots. The moment he saw his friend, he remembered that Menne had lived in this building. "Man, there ain't much left, is there?" The greeting sounded more cordial than he had intended. "Hell, no," said Menne. "Do you know, sometimes I sit here, thinking: I did Latin — this must have been my room, remember? — and math and all, and now I'm here again, but everything else is gone. My parents, too."

Bernd fished out a pack of Camels with three cigarettes in it. He couldn't think of anything to say. They laughed, smoked, slapped each other on the back. There was so much to say that they couldn't say anything. Two years had passed and a world had come to an end. They slid off the charred wall where they were sitting, wandered aimlessly into the desert of ruins, into a cellar filled with the smell, so familiar to Bernd, of damp mortar and cloying rot. With the same movement they both unbuttoned their trousers at the same moment. When they had finished, Menne said: "Did you do it too for a cigarette in your camp? The one who could do it first and farthest got a cigarette." "Menne, man, I wasn't in a camp, you know that. But where I was the one who was done first got a slice of bread and lard, or he'd be excused from making the rounds and climbing up on the roof when there was a raid." "Bernd, man, talking about school — you know what, it seems they're going to open our old school again in the old girls' school over by the S-Bahn bridge. What do you say? How about we go over there tomorrow and take a look? I think it's getting boring all the time without school. What about you?" Bernd was thrilled. He was delighted to have run into Menne. Maybe he'd be seeing some of the others, Ralph or Günter, "the Sash," who wagged his ass when he walked and was always first in geography. Menne was living with relatives, so they arranged to meet the next day.

That afternoon Bernd heard at the "bazaar" that a black company was moving into the old brick building by the General Pape Strasse S-Bahn station.

Bernd had never seen a black man in all his life. He was sorry he had made the date with Menne.

The school was really about to reopen. There were no regular classes, and so far there were only three teachers, but one of these was Bernd's and Menne's class teacher. He had only one arm left and he was very glad to see the two emaciated faces that had turned up so unexpectedly. Pupils and teachers decided that school should start the following Monday. That left Bernd four days for expeditions to the black continent.

The smell, the sounds, the movement, all were strange. Everything was shabby and run-down in the makeshift barracks beside the S-Bahn tracks, even the weapons, uniforms, and vehicles looked secondhand. But Bernd was in seventh heaven. The blacks were bigger and noisier than he had expected. They had painted everything in bright colors. What he heard through the clatter of the mess hall, "Chattanooga Choo Choo" and "Gonna take a sentimental journey, gonna put my heart at ease," at once happy and sorrowful, had no connection with anything he had ever heard before. The words were beyond him, but he understood. Instinctively. Here there was warmth, friendliness, and a searing hatred that changed the soldiers' faces beyond recognition when an officer hove in sight. Gone was the easygoing friendliness. The officers were white.

Bernd took it all in. The skin was lighter on the palms of their hands. They had a different way of going down the stairs, their feet slanting rather than lengthwise. When they laughed, they laughed. They sang. One of them took hold of Bernd's reddish brown hair, put it down on his own black forearm, laughed with pleasure at the impossible color combination, and gave Bernd a can of peanuts. Only the Russians had *given* him something, those unpoisoned cookies that had tasted as strange as these bitter, salty nuts that everything here seemed to smell of. Even the brown paste they spread on their enormous slabs of white bread had the same taste, though it was also a bit musty. But good. Bernd liked everything, and the blacks liked him from the first. They adopted him, a puppy, a mascot. They took him into their barracks — the sentries only saluted — where they didn't have rooms with two beds like the Amis in the school building, but big dormitories crowded with cots made up with scratchy woolen blankets, where everything stank of oil. It was a transportation unit, and oily rags and stained brown tennis shoes were lying all around.

The very first day they hid Bernd in the dormitory and after dinner each of the black giants brought some leftovers in a flat mess kit divided into sections, which reminded him of the "merry-go-round," a turntable with crystal compartments on which Irmchen had served salads at her dinner parties. The American merry-go-rounds were made of olive green tin; in one section there were cubes of some orange-yellow vegetable, in another bright yellow kernels, and Jimmy, Bernd's first friend, brought him a whole mess kit full of chicken and rice in a spicy green-and-yellow sauce. Bernd had never eaten yams, sweet corn, or curried chicken — but he took an instant liking to them. Nobody laughed at him, nobody flicked cigarettes at him, nobody offered him prechewed chewing gum. Only Jimmy, the smallest and ugliest of them, always vivacious and sometimes aggressive, took the cigarette out of Bernd's mouth. "How old are you?" he asked. "Fifteen," Bernd lied, but Jimmy didn't believe him. Then, realizing that he had hurt Bernd's feelings, he gave him a cake of Palmolive soap.

With that priceless treasure Bernd came home. He didn't want to talk about his experience. He felt too strongly about it, best keep it to himself for a while. The cake of soap was enough for his father. He hadn't expected explanations in a long time; they would have meant much less than the smell of the soap to his feverish brain. His tuberculosis was corroding him from within. He still resisted the pain of his coughing fits, but not the oncoming of death. He spread out pictures on his gray coverlet, all of himself: as a lieutenant on horseback, sporting a tennis racket, in swimming trunks on the lake shore, on the Baltic beach, sticking little flags into a sand castle. The film of his life was running backward, but even that he had ceased to understand. He hung shriveled in the web of a gray, tormented past, impervious to the present. His mind wandered, he talked incoherent nonsense, often in Russian or French. The Sparrow listened as she flitted about, and explained to Bernd that in his delirious mouthings scenes from the prison camp seemed to be mixed up with memories of his meeting with Bernd's mother, all as real and as unreal as the reddish X-ray twilight in the room and the strangely bright orange-red streaks of blood and foam that trickled down the invalid's now wholly white beard. The only realities now were the urinal, the commode, and the scraps from the black soldiers' mess hall that fed the retired major general's household.

At first Bernd said nothing about his home life to his new friends. They filled his belly, and he wouldn't have wanted to steal from them. It was Jimmy who sensed that something was wrong — one day when he was showing Bernd some photographs of a wretched hovel with a lot of black people, "the family," in front of it. They looked happy, but looking at these laughing people so far away, Bernd felt his heart sink. That night he had no desire to play the interpreter; he had advanced to that function, mouthpiece of a barter economy. He had mastered the technical vocabulary and had learned to translate sentences such as "I want to fuck you" or "Ask her if she'll suck my cock" into good commercial German. "Three packs of Lucky Strikes for a lay," "A carton of cigarettes for a blow job," and so on. The girls, some of whom he had known wearing the green-and-black or red-and-white cordon of a troop leader, could now be recognized by their bright-colored Ami silk scarves. At sundown quite a few of them would flock to the barracks of the black company. Sex was a cut-and-dried business proposition. That didn't bother Bernd unless they giggled too much or gave themselves airs or threatened to run away.

That night he was in no mood for pimping. He told his story in his broken English, and after that he had no need to fish bread and peanut butter soaked in a mixture of coffee and cocoa out of the big corrugated-iron cans that looked like gas-mask containers. The next morning Jimmy pulled up in front of the *Yuricke* in a gigantic army truck and handed the horrified Sparrow a big package.

At that hour Bernd was already in school. He had an exacting schedule: up at five, dash to the black barracks, back home with a container of cocoa and a mess kit full of ham and eggs, his father's breakfast; then to school. He had got what he wanted: no more sleeping in the sickroom; the whole day from morning to night belonged to him. His father was feeling better, no doubt, Bernd felt sure, because of the improvement in his diet. And another thing: Bernd usually had enough cigarettes to exchange on the black market for codeine, his father's only medicine. What Bernd didn't know was that at that stage of the disease "feeling better" was a sure sign that death was near. Bernd had no idea of what tuberculosis was; the word was unknown to him; his father was sick, he had a cough, that was all; he'd be OK, as Bernd had learned to say; death was outside his sphere of experience. Somehow life was going on. He was only fourteen; an ocean of time lay ahead of him; his imagination, his energy, his toughened will to live were all oriented toward the future. There was no stopping, no turning or even looking back. The world was in ruins, but with the resilience of a hungry cat he had clawed his way out of the wreckage and saved his tattered, burnt, scabby skin. Now it was smoothing out. He didn't know all this, because he didn't think about his life, he lived it. He rushed from place to place, driven by hunger and curiosity. In these postwar summer months he had acquired a face. The fat, undersized little boy with the round head, protruding ears, and big eyes had become a strong, wiry youngster, who had no control over his mop of chestnut brown hair and didn't know that his greenish blue eyes were attractive. He wasn't vain. He was glad when he detected the first light fuzz on his upper lip. Otherwise he had no perception of himself.

The mails were working again. A card came from a village in the Harz Mountains, the first news in months. Irmfried had run away from the Russians and was living in the British zone. "I'm well," she wrote. No questions about anyone else.

The Sparrow was beginning to bellyache. Her face had always had the expression of a nibbling rabbit; ever since the Russians had stolen her monkey

THE SURVIVOR

jacket and there was no dye available for her bun, the nibbling had become a baring of teeth. Now there was something furtive and lurking about her look. "A skinned rabbit," Bernd thought. With the quiet fervent obstinacy of a nun panting under her monstrance, she clung to two eminently petit bourgeois traits. She was complacently avid for praise, and she was assiduous at looking out for herself. Whatever she did, she commented on it and — blinking her eyelashless eyes — expected due praise from others. "See how I've darned the stockings," she would say. "It wasn't easy getting hold of darning wool." Or "Look what I've made. This rice will last us two days. It was very hard to cook it up again. Your aunt has made a good job of it, hasn't she?" Even harder to bear was her concern for her own comfort and well-being. "I can't go out today. The wind is too cold"; "My shoulders ache from chopping parsley"; "My cough kept me awake all night." Bernd had once suggested to his sister that they should keep a catalog of the Sparrow's complaints, which they had long quoted and parodied. One was "The bristles of my toothbrush cut me badly this morning." "I'll remember that one as long as I live," said Hermine.

Now the Sparrow claimed to have been infected by her brother. Her almost daily greeting was: "I've been spitting blood all morning." She was standing at the kitchen sink and, true enough, the water was tinged with blood, caused, however, by ill-fitting dentures. A good Samaritan she was not. Because of her allegedly failing health, she demanded Irmfried's immediate return. "When will you make your wife come home? Her place is with her sick husband. Why should she be sitting around in Clausthal? There's nothing to stop her from traveling. She's in the West zone same as we are. You can see that I'm almost at the end of my rope, I'm sacrificing myself, I really ought to be in a home, there are homes for unmarried pastor's daughters, you know." She nagged and complained and left the sick man no peace. "Why in God's name doesn't she come home?" The old man summoned up his strength and wrote to Irmchen that he was ill and that she was urgently needed. She wrote back on a postcard from the Harz Mountains: "Go to the hospital if you're sick." Outrage gave the old man new strength. He initiated divorce proceedings.

The winter was over. Bernd had bought a tile stove for his father's room and discovered too late that it was an ornamental object and that any attempt to make a fire in it released dense clouds of smoke. Since the cold brought on coughing fits, the stove was used, but the smoke was even worse than the cold for the old man's tortured lungs. So a small cylindrical stove supplied by Jimmy was moved into the sickroom. Icicles formed in the other rooms. Bernd went to bed with a seltzer siphon full of hot water. He inadvertently activated the siphon with his big toe, creating a puddle in his bed that froze solid before morning. Just once he got hold of some coal. He discovered a big pile of anthracite in a railroad yard, jealously guarded by military police. Thieving had become second nature with him and he hummed the song hit: "No fire, no love, no coal so hard, As coal that's swiped from a railroad yard." He figured it was reserved for the always-overheated Ami barracks. Jimmy and his friends helped him. One night with a forged pass they drove an eighteen-ton truck from the army motor pool into the railroad yard. They left the motor running, turned the radio up full blast, blew the horn furiously, and staged a simulated fight. Whistles, shouts: "What's going on?" "What are you doing here? Get out, you no-good bastards. Let's go, let's go!" Meanwhile, Bernd loaded a full sack of coal onto his sled and, by then as black as his friends, disappeared. Coughing and shivering with fear, he rubbed more and more coal dust into his eyes. Dragging his screeching sled, he passed his father's old beer saloon. Now it was a "club" and brightly lit. Gusts of music and laughter poured through the swing door. The place exuded warmth and well-being. Big chrome-plated cars with flashing teeth in their well-fed faces were parked outside. A wave of hate poured over Bernd. Taking a run as on a toboggan slide, he rammed his coal sled into the Chryslers and Packards and Chevrolets — mudguards, headlights, taillights, whatever it happened to hit. Snot, sweat, and tears mixed with coal dust gave him a hideous mask as he danced behind his kamikaze sled. "Me too!" The words passed through his brain in bursts. "Metoometoometoo. I'm sick of being cold and hungry and eating peanut butter. I want bright lights, warmth, and laughter." He wanted happiness, though he didn't know it.

Father's Death

The postcard brought a bit of happiness. The Snail! From the Snail. It was spring. Bernd had completely forgotten his birthday and was startled by his father's unusually early call. When he went into the sickroom, the old man was shaking, racked by a coughing fit. Two little stones fell to the floor. His father's dress cufflinks of black onyx — his birthday present to his fifteen-year-old son. In the afternoon, Fräulein Wilhelm, Herr Walther's vivacious, smartly dressed secretary, dropped in. She had often been to see them, and both children were fond of her. She brought the postcard; it was addressed to her, but meant for Bernd. "Dear Coweyes, I'm in Berlin. I haven't forgotten you. Happy birthday."

Away he went. Without a word, on his recently "modernized" bicycle. To the despair of his teachers he had mounted a stolen dynamo-powered car radio on the handlebars. "I have to take it to class with me; if I didn't, it'd be gone before you could hear a pig squeal"; such expressions infuriated the teachers, especially the elderly English teacher, who knew perfectly well that fear for the bicycle's safety was a pretext and that Bernd's real purpose was to lift the hind wheel, whirl the pedals, and play boogie-woogie, to the delight of his classmates. Altogether, the Oxford-educated gentleman was none too pleased with Walther, Bernd, who would brazenly flaunt a pack of Camels or nonchalantly announce: "Sorry, I can't come tomorrow, I must go to the black market to feed my family." Not to mention the bitter battles over the English language. By that time Bernd spoke rather fluently, but his teacher refused to recognize as English such locutions as "I ain't hungry" or "I gotta go." When Bernd solemnly asked him: "Could you explain to me what 'gonna' means?" the teacher fell into the trap and replied: "There is no such word in the English language." Quick as a flash, Bernd came back at him: "Perhaps I can help you there. It means 'going to . . .' For instance, in the song: 'Gonna take a sentimental journey . . .'" He enjoyed tormenting this teacher. All the teachers for that matter. Except a young assistant teacher of history (she called it "social studies") and a young pastor, who turned up once a week on a bicycle and gave religious instruction but didn't seem the least bit "pious." There was something tantalizing about the history teacher, there was talk of some tragedy in her life. As for the pastor, he made a big hit with the boys by inviting them to a lecture on love and sex at the parsonage.

Away Bernd went on his bicycle. In one hand, like a flag, the postcard with the address: Reichskanzlerplatz 7, Berlin-Charlottenburg. He'd never heard of any Reichskanzlerplatz. "Oh, that must be Adolf-Hitlerplatz," someone finally told him. He crossed the whole city with his lucky flag, dancing a glittering chrome-and-steel boogie-woogie past street after street of gaping ruins. There wasn't any Reichskanzlerplatz 7, only a heap of rubble.

It was late that night when he got home. His head pounded, his hands were ice-cold, and he was dog-tired. One of his tires had gone flat and he had pushed most of the way. His nose was running.

But a week later Fräulein Wilhelm was back again. The Snail had been to see her. "Not a word to the old man. I want nothing to do with him. Only Coweyes. What's Coweyes doing?"

It was a large, once upper-class apartment house on Kaisersdamm, only a few steps away from the wrong address that Hermine had written on her postcard. Bernd knew such houses from visits to friends of his father's. He disliked them, their big lobbies with mirrors and little marble benches and carpeted corridors and elevators with bird and flower designs on their doors. Everything about them sounded hollow, had a musty smell and a rusty taste. To his amazement, the whole building seemed intact. Up until then he had known only ruins, half-ruins, and houses stripped to the bone by looters.

The door was decorated with half-naked wooden water nymphs. To ring the bell one manipulated the tongue of a bronze lion. Years after he had rung, he heard steps. In the interval, thousands of little explosions had evoked bright, sharp, fugitive images: magnesium flares, the so-called "Christmas trees" dropped by British planes; the three of them dragging sacks through the tunnel under the Görlitz railroad station; the Snail with her makeup kit on the way to the air-raid shelter; arguments about the BBC broadcasts over the ivory-colored radio; his father's cries of "My pistol! Where's my pistol?" in the foundering *Yuricke*; the Snail in her bloodstained muslin nightgown, slobbering Biomalt; the Asiatic Russian with the walrus mustache.

The door, flanked by two huntresses aiming plaster spears at the bronze lion, opened, and out came a Russian in uniform. An officer with slanting Asiatic eyes and a black walrus mustache. The mustache was smaller, but then the man himself was smaller. A cloud of thick black mucus rose from Bernd's stomach to his head. All he could think through it was: "Why is he so little?" He heard a voice coated with bitter mucus say in English: "My name is Bernd Walther." Then he began to cry.

Farther back, at the end of a long corridor, a door opened. There stood his sister in a dressing gown, half combed and half made-up. After a long hug they sat on the sofa in the large, expensively furnished room. To one side, on a small table, he saw the silver frame from their father's desk, and in it a childhood picture of brother and sister, she strikingly blonde and he all eyes. Bernd had never noticed that she had taken the framed picture away with her. Of course, it had proved impossible to go traveling through Germany a month after the capitulation. The four of them had got as far as the Elbe and not a step further. René and the German pilot with the forged English passport had been allowed to cross over, she and Ani had been sent back. Ani knew of a pension on Kaisersdamm, but when the Snail went to inquire about a room, the apartment had been commandeered by the Russian communications officer in charge of Radio Berlin, who was living there with his aide-de-camp. That was the little Asiatic at the door. "Kolya is entirely different, he's big and blond, he could be mistaken for a German." Kolya, Major Nikolenko, was Hermine's lover.

At first Bernd couldn't take it all in. This big, fancy apartment, his sister, who now made the impression of a grown woman, Kolya, who joined them later in the evening, young, ever so slender, crew cut and gnawed fingernails, almost perfect German, soft-spoken, friendly. He seemed worried about something, but grew wildly festive when he heard it was Bernd's birthday. Guests arrived, food was served, salt herring and succulent sausage, some kind of vegetable soup, vodka, and sweet champagne — from the Crimea, someone said. Bernd had no idea what the Crimea might be, nor did he understand the language, which to his surprise his sister spoke with apparent ease. The warmth, for which he had longed, and the pungent foreign atmosphere made him feel foggy. This party was something like the ones at home long ago. Here again there was loud music, dancing, liquor, and a lot of strangers, whirling excitedly around. But these people didn't laugh at him, let alone send him to bed. They thought it odd that he insisted on talking English. "I take it that your brother is Mr. Bevin,"* said one of them. That was their way of making a fuss over him.

Next morning his head was bursting. The apartment was quiet, no one was there. He stayed in his sister's bed and dozed and waited. It was almost noon when she came home. "I'm sorry. I have my interpreters' school in the morning." Bernd had to go home; never before had he stayed out all night.

His abrupt explanation sufficed: "Hermine is coming home next week," he told his father. "She has a Russian friend now, something to do with the radio, but she'll be living here again. We'll move into your old study together, we'll fix it up somehow." Hermine had suggested this arrangement when Bernd told her what it was like in the house. On the

---

*Ernest Bevin (1881–1951), British labor statesman and Foreign Secretary, 1945–1951.

following Monday Kolya brought her home in his old BMW. He carried her trunk to the door, but declined to come in; Hermine had no doubt told him too much about her father, and the young Soviet Russian had no desire to meet the dying old German officer.

Hermine arrived just five days before Irmfried. The district court had sent the divorce petition to Clausthal, and a reply was not long in coming: "Arrive Saturday. Irmfried." Bernd was glad he didn't have to face this family reunion alone. With various odds and ends of furniture, he and Hermine built themselves a hideaway, a little place of their own. The library was their bedroom, where they lay side by side chattering half the night, and the adjoining room, for which there was not quite enough furniture, their living room.

"Irmchen, dear child" moved in with an incredible quantity of luggage, cartons, crates, suitcases, bales of goods. "Well, children, you needn't tell Wotan, but I've been having a wonderful time. You know I can sew a little. So I sewed and washed clothes for the Tommies. The whole meadow in front of the house was littered with empty cheese boxes and cartons of cigarettes. The fat of the land, I tell you, the fat of the land! And those clean young boys!" She laughed as if she had bitten into a juicy steak. She looked as if she had just come back from a vacation. She had brought mounds of provisions and cooked two meals a day — for herself. For her dying husband, nothing. On the third day she said to the children: "Let Hermine's Ivan worry about him. A pretty young girl's got to be crazy running around with a Russian these days. Aren't there enough Amis?" So Bernd kept going to his blacks. But sometimes Hermine took him with her to Kaisersdamm, where they ate sumptuously and drank, drank, drank. Hermine absolutely forbade Bernd to take anything home with him, even a slice of sausage or a herring. "Coweyes!" she fumed. "Are you crazy?" when she caught him in the kitchen, starting to wrap something up while the Russians in the big dining room were carousing with music and candles and whole batteries of bottles. "It's out of the question. No scrounging around here. I'm not accepting any presents, either!" "The Snail is nuts," said Ani, who was working at the English NAAFI* Club and was able to do a flourishing business selling the articles she "put aside" on the black market. "That hideous junk that Kolya brings her, that green blouse for instance, she'll never be able to wear it."

Hermine was taking no presents. But neither was she letting anything be taken from her. For years there had been no love lost between her and her stepmother, and now they hated each other fiercely. Hermine distrusted Irmfried's dealings with her father's lawyer. Surprisingly, the old man suddenly

---

*Navy, Army, and Airforce Institutes. An organization providing canteens, shops, etc., for British military personnel.

recovered energy enough to listen to his daughter's misgivings. "Divorcing her isn't enough," said Hermine. "You've got to disinherit her, and make sure she doesn't get to be our guardian. We're both minors. You've got to attend to that, Papa."

And so, unbeknownst to the stewing, roasting, and frying stepmother, a will was drawn up. Bernd was too busy seesawing between vodka and peanut butter to hear much about it. But one afternoon brought an unexpected complication. His father called him in: "Bernd-Jörn, you're a big boy now. You probably have a girlfriend?" Bernd didn't know which nettled him more, his father's prurient curiosity or the fact that he didn't have a girlfriend. He took walks with "Honeybee"; that was Sabine, the younger sister of a former HY Leader, with whom he had become acquainted long ago on the athletic field. They often went walking in the evening on the narrow overgrown paths that paralleled the gardens of the less-prosperous houses. Now and then he stole fruit or flowers for her, but he never felt much like kissing her, though she gave him ample opportunity. Recently at a party to celebrate one of her girlfriends' engagement to an Ami — she was seriously planning to go to America with him — some liqueur that tasted like peppermint had made him very sick to his stomach. He didn't know which disgusted him more, the smooching or that sticky, bitter goo. Was it any of the old man's business?

"Oh, well, you don't have to answer that, my

FATHER'S DEATH

boy." What was he getting at with this "my boy"? "But just be careful, diseases are the worst thing that can happen to you. And that's not all. In the army we used to say, when the cock stands up, the brain lies down." The old man was off again on his stupid army memories that didn't interest Bernd in the least. And why this "Bernd-Jörn" routine? "You've got to be on your guard against two things. Don't catch the clap. And don't play with yourself. We had one of those in our company. He used to do it in bed at night. One night we pulled off his blanket, and there it was in all its glory. Ha-ha-ha."

A giggling, slavering death's-head, but the eyes were surprisingly clear and kindly, despite the barrackroom slobber that was pouring out of the mouth. Bernd was touched by the friendliness he read in his father's eyes. "Yes, Papa," he said. Meaningless words, but they brought the old man back to the present. He smacked his forehead and smiled sheepishly, as though to ask forgiveness. The smile made his face entirely different. "I've made my will. Cutting Irmfried out. Everything goes to you children. But I can't think of a guardian for you. Bernd-Jörn, I'm going to die — very soon — and I don't know who'll look after you. All my friends are in the West."

This was getting on Bernd's nerves. He had a date with Honeybee; he wanted to go out. He couldn't bear his father's helplessness, the imploring tone of his "I'm going to die." He failed to see that this had anything to do with him. Yet he was sensitive to the tortured seriousness with which his father had spoken. "Why not take our pastor at school?" he suggested. "He's a good sort, he's young, and I get along with him."

To Honeybee he didn't say a word about his father. He stole pears from the lady teacher's garden. He thought he had seen her at her window in her nightgown. In her nightgown in the afternoon. He knew what that meant. Well, he didn't *know*, but he could imagine.

It must have been last year's pears hanging on the tree. When he bit into one, it was tasty, hard, slightly sour, at once bitter and sweet. Delicious but inedible. It was a quince. The next time their stepmother started frying her detested bacon, brother and sister smirked. "I see something you don't see. It ends in . . . double *l*." Their alliance had been reinforced by an unexpected blow. One morning Irmfried had come out of the sickroom holding a handkerchief over her face. "You've seen me, you'll have to testify, I've spent the night with Wotan." Neither Bernd nor Hermine could see the point. Up until then Irmfried had never spent more than a few minutes in the sickroom — "I can hardly bear going to the toilet myself," she said. A few days later it came out. According to the law, divorce proceedings were nullified if the couple spent a night together after they were initiated. It would be necessary to start all over again, and for that Friedrich-Wilhelm Walther no longer had the strength.

One evening in the Kaisersdamm apartment, the Snail whispered in Bernd's ear: "We're doing all right. It's signed and sealed, she's been disinherited and disqualified." They hugged and kissed and danced around the huge apartment. Kolya was amused. Head over heels in love with Hermine, he had become attached to her brother. "We're almost like a family," he would say, always on a note of sadness. That evening Bernd shoveled in food indiscriminately, played "Mr. Bevin," spoke English, and mixed vodka cocktails. Hermine wore the aide's uniform, gave herself slit eyes with an eyebrow pencil, put on heavy boots, and stamped out a polka with her hands on her hips. Bernd only knew the fox-trot, but he joined in; he danced with Kolya, with the Asiatic aide, who with only a pajama jacket on was taking fruit out of a big crystal bowl and throwing it around the room. The table was littered with fish bones and scraps of bread and cheese, all awash in vodka. Kolya brought in a little brown suitcase and emptied it over Bernd, candy, hundreds of candies in green and red and pink and yellow paper. They danced the candy to smithereens, licked the bones and threw fruit at one another, and all smoked Russian *papirossi* with triangular-folded mouthpieces. Deep in the night the old BMW drove brother and sister home. The Snail whispered in his ear: "I see something you don't see — it ends in ... double *l*. Man, Coweyes, the will." Naked and sweaty, happy and deeply afraid, they crawled into bed and held each other tight.

Hermine woke him up in the gray of dawn. She was sitting beside him on the bed, bathed in tears, shaken with sobs. "Papa is dead." She couldn't be comforted and she wouldn't answer questions. "I know it. He's dead. I just know. Stupid Coweyes. Don't ask such stupid questions. He's dead. Can't you get it through your head? Dead."

They ran down the stairs, forgetting that they were naked. Ran into their father's room, the ghost room, the hemorrhage room, the black-lung room. The early-morning light shone through the reddish violet X-ray windowpanes. He had shaken his covers off, and there he lay, glassy-eyed, his face overlaid with the reflection of a misshapen stomach, a hole where the teeth in his gaping mouth seemed to be eating it, his gaunt fingers inextricably intertwined, a skeleton. Friedrich-Wilhelm Walther, bank president and retired major general. His sister took the ridiculous green silk ribbon out of her hair and tied it around his head to keep his mouth closed. He looked silly, a pale Easter egg with a green bow. Bernd shed no tears.

Strangely Together

The Snail was gone. Bernd had no way of knowing whether it was the realization of this sudden finality or the strange out-of-the-worldness of the military railroad station that set his head spinning and made him feel as if he were at the movies. This had no connection with the everyday world as he knew it, this gleaming, immaculate train with sleeping compartments, mahogany doors with brass fittings, a dining car, baskets of bread and fruit on white tablecloths, and little bottles of wine in ringlike holders. Women with the recently created New Look, in high-heeled cork sandalettes or thick-soled pumps protruding from under ankle-length coats or skirts, with fur pieces or capes over square, martial-looking shoulders, accompanied by officers of various nations, armies, and branches of service. Chauffeurs had unloaded luggage from jeeps, Buicks, and Peugeots and stowed it away. Bernd had had to repress an automatic impulse when he saw half-smoked cigarettes being flicked away.

That gleaming monster had carried the Snail away. On her legs the living room chandelier, on her head the refrigerator — in other words, nylons with seams and a chic little fur cap. She was wearing half the living room furniture, and the soft leather chairs from the library were stowed away in the luggage compartment, having been metamorphosed via cartons of Camels into leather suitcases of the same color. Through his tears Bernd saw everything double and transmogrified — overlaid by memory, fear, and wild images of a glittering Paris — the plundered house, the Snail's wine-colored floor-length coat, for which he personally had brought his Leica to barrel-assed Emmi on Olivaer Platz, to the windowless "Berlin room"* of that affable but relentless bargainer, who held state amidst pails of honey, cartons of cigarettes, mounds of sausages, cartons of soap and Hershey bars, a calculating fairy godmother. It was like the movie he had seen with the Snail only last week, Jean Cocteau's *La Belle et la Bête* — his perception dispersed into multiple reflections. They stood face-to-face in silence; everything had been said. The Snail looked as if she had already been

---

*Many Berlin apartments had a windowless room of this kind, which thus came to be known jocosely as a "Berliner Zimmer."

carried away — and yet she kept casting nervous glances in the direction of her compartment. Bernd felt that everything was being taken from him — and yet he wished this gleaming goddess would finally be gone.

The Snail was gone. Bernd was hungry. He picked up a cigarette butt. He didn't know exactly where he was — they had come in a taxi, but there weren't any taxis here, it wasn't an ordinary railroad station, and he had no idea where the nearest U-Bahn or S-Bahn station might be. He was thirsty. He knew there was a bit of vodka left in the house — the Cocteau film tore, or maybe it was over. Just as at the movies the viewer's dream is invariably followed by "The End," the velvet curtain, and a scrabbling for handbags, coats, and scarves — the gangplank back to reality — so Bernd was shaken out of his daze by a screeching of tires, the slamming of a car door, and the clatter of heavy boots: Kolya.

There he was. Hideous meaningless red carnations sticking out of the *Pravda*. His face was empty, a sleepwalker with open, tear-filled eyes. Not a word. He grabbed Bernd's head, a bristling woolly crutch. Turning around, they made for the BMW that Bernd so enviously admired. "Let's go," said Kolya. That's all he was capable of saying. He offered the driver a *papirossa*, something he would never have done under ordinary circumstances. All three smoked until they reached the empty house.

Empty and toothless. In the living room there was

still a couch, a little low table, and the peeling sideboard. They too had been sold, but the compassionate black marketeer had agreed not to pick them up for two or three days. The driver carried Kolya's inevitable suitcase in. Two big bottles of vodka, smoked fish, salami, grapes, and cigarettes. There were still glasses on the table. One was stained with lipstick. Bernd and Kolya exchanged glances. Bernd took the glass and gave it to Kolya.

They were soon drunk. Then at last the dam burst. An incomprehensible flood of words burst from Kolya; his speech became more and more jerky and disjointed, as if his German had forsaken him. Shit. Toolate. Whydidn'twe? Neverevernothing. Ifonlywehadn't. Forbiddenforbiddenforbidden. Germanrussiannazis. Berlinhalleparis. Gone. Neverneveragain.

Bernd had no need to translate. He knew. Russian soldiers were forbidden to fraternize with German women. Despite every possible precaution it was bound to come out, Soviet officers stationed in West Berlin were under special surveillance. Nikolai had been transferred to Halle. Berlinhalleparis. Officially this was not a punitive measure, but then he had been notified that he would soon be ordered home to Kiev. Whenever he could, he had found a pretext for a weekend in Berlin; when that proved impossible, the Snail had gone to Halle. Dark visits — before nightfall Kolya would unscrew the light bulb in the elevator; in the apartment they had to be as still as mice, they could never leave the house together, and even separately they avoided going out in the daytime. As Kolya couldn't disappear for a whole weekend, Hermine often had to wait for hours in the gloomy requisitioned apartment until he — usually pretending to be drunk — managed to tear himself away from his fellow officers. On Monday before daybreak the Snail would make her way to the station, where she would have to wait for as much as five hours — since the Berlin train, when there was one, didn't leave until almost noon. Eighteen hours on a wooden bench in an unheated car for eight hours of love. Berlinhalleparis. Bernd knew the meaning of Kolya's disjointed words. The Berlin–Paris military train passed through Halle.

The two of them sat exhausted on the ragged couch. Behind them woolen blankets embroidered with ridiculous pseudoarabesques, supported by what was left of the wire mesh from the old plaster partitions separating the living room from the kitchen. Before them on the cracked glass tabletop, looking like the bottom of an overturned aquarium displaying drowned fishes, brown and oily, their lashless, expressionless eyes staring out of shrouds printed in Cyrillic letters, their tiny, razor-sharp teeth biting on useless pickle-slice life preservers. On the floor lay Kolya's sweat-drenched jacket with the epaulets and pistol belt. Beside it his red-star cap full of salami and matches — the shopping bag of postwar Berlin. The twenty-eight-year-old from

Kiev, tank driver, Germanist, radio station administrator, Hermine's lover, momentarily in the house of the late consumptive general, was slight and frail, more boy than grown man. His heavy growth of beard looked manly enough, but the curly down on his chest, now wet and cottony, was that of an adolescent.

Bernd was hungry. Mechanically, he stuffed on smoked herring, grapes, salami, and pickles, pausing now and then for a slug of vodka. Kolya drank. He drained glass after glass, and when he let go the glass it was only to fold the mouthpiece of the next *papirossa* — once lengthwise, once crosswise. His fingertips were burnt brown from the countless defective matches that broke off or burned too quickly or fizzled out. It was ice-cold in the room; no one had thought of making a fire, and they shivered and perspired at once. They didn't talk. Bernd sat bolt upright, his head in a fog. He saw nothing unusual when Kolya pissed out the window, just looked sleepily at the pathetically thin naked man in the purplish evening glow of the X-ray windowpanes, a living skeleton with a framed one behind it. The victorious tank driver.

The first shot shook Bernd out of his torpor. He wasn't surprised, it was as though he had been expecting it. Kolya stood swaying beside the little table covered with fish bones, greasy paper, and pieces of pickle floating in vodka. Each of his hands had a life of its own. With the right he shot at the chandelier, with the left he stroked the curly thicket between his legs. Bernd had never seen him naked, he was amazed at his wild hairy bush — a gutted horsehair cushion with a penis hanging out of it. But then he was diverted by a horrible thought: the baroque chandelier with the art deco base had been sold for eight chocolate bars, five packages of pudding powder, and a carton of Chesterfields; he was supposed to "deliver" that chandelier in three days.

A fish bone between his teeth had cut his tongue; was that where the blood came from, or was it from the hot pepper? But then he remembered that he had bitten his lips on the station platform. Without a word he takes the pistol from the hand of the reeling Russian and fires. Absently, as though lost in thought, Kolya strokes his fur animal and throws his arm around Bernd and guides his pistol-firing hand. The chandelier had twenty-four arms, but only four bulbs. When three had been knocked out, someone pounded on the door. It was "Irmchen, dear child," shivering, grotesque under a thick layer of facial cream, a torn woolen blanket over her shoulders. "God almighty, what's going on, are you trying to kill me, you're shooting through the ceiling..." She stops short, a clock with a broken spring — she has caught sight of the frail naked Russian, his hair-stroking hand and the gun in Bernd's hand. Bernd is a hostage to sadness and anger. She slams the door and screams: "If there's any more shooting, I'm getting out of here" — a statement as absurd as everything else that has been said and done that evening. Far from sobering Bernd, the incident has thrown him into a cold, avenging rage. Kolya has to hold him to keep him from running after her with the gun. Kolya's grip becomes an embrace. Trembling in the damp cold they caress each other. They slump down on the decrepit couch, two plucked, exhausted, shivering fighting cocks, and cover themselves with Kolya's overcoat. Bobbing and pitching, the *Yuricke* carries them through the night. The heavy coat is a greenish brown sail; the deck below it smells of the Snail, of fish, and then some. Kolya's kiss is bitter, fibrous, thin. *Machorka*, cucumber, vodka, beard stubble. Kolya jumps up, shoots off his gun until the magazine is empty, laughs. His laughter cracks, the next-to-last shot hits the light bulb, the sound of splintered wood ties Bernd's befuddled brain into a ball. Baroque-furryanimal-gun.

In, over, and under each other. The *Yuricke* is sinking, they are each other's planks. Snail plank, Bernd plank, hair pistol, steel furry animal, splintering hips, taffrail, hair cables, skin wood, wave swell spray yearning grief hate loneliness oblivion. Suspicion. Strangely together. Warm in affliction. Deadly alive.

Dream Hands

Every plank had gone down. Bernd struggled from eddy to eddy. Frantic to survive, he swam without direction. He saw the thawing rim of the ice floe. Wet, exhausted, panic-stricken, he searched for a dry warm corner. He was sixteen.

The house was gone with all its "innards," as they had cheerfully called the furniture and other accessories when selling them piece by piece on the black market. From the refrigerator to the chandelier, from the (phony) Renaissance bookcase to the mangle — everything had been unloaded. The final paroxysm had been the grand auction. This was their triumphant revenge. Not only had they flung all these possessions away, torn the scabs off their wounds once and for all; what's more, they had done it in secret, for both brother and sister were minors, forbidden to dispose of anything whatsoever with-

THE SURVIVOR

out the approval of their guardian. Suddenly the pastor Bernd had picked, idolized until only recently, now an enemy, was in the way. Brother and sister would have found a world without an enemy unlivable. They had literally shut the door on the young theologian, who despite having two children of his own had been unable to gainsay the wish of a dying man. When they needed him, when, for instance, the electricity company threatened to shut off their current, they would arrange to meet him at the bank or at the parsonage. Sometimes the man would bicycle out to the house, which had been thoroughly gutted, even the frames of the double windows had been removed and sold, and then brother and sister would take pleasure in pretending not to hear him ring and watching him through a slit in the blinds. The auction had been a great event, because they had prevailed on "the Sash" to preside. That was Bernd's school friend, the effeminate youngster who swayed his hips when he walked, a favorite with Bernd because their parents, Bernd's father and the Sash's mother, had forbidden them to have anything to do with each other. They would remove some of the notices thumbtacked to trees along the street — "Handcart for sale," "Wish to buy ladies' bicycle," "Wish to exchange acetylene blowtorch for sunlamp" — and in their place pin messages to each other: "Meet me at 4 in park shelter" or "Will not be in math class tomorrow." The Sash was off-limits. Great!

Now in white tennis trousers and a checked shirt out of a CARE package, he was auctioning off the rest of their belongings — the last couch, the glass-topped table, a vacuum cleaner. He waved the gavel like a fan, rolled his eyes, and wagged his ass. He was astonishingly successful, taking in almost a hundredweight of white flour.

All that was in the past. The Sash had even auctioned off the "second-class" sofa, so-called because it was upholstered with the same olive green rep as the second-class compartments in German trains and also reminded Bernd of the curtains in Fräulein Wilhelm's office. Bernd had bored a hole in the frayed, rotting rep, crammed it with horsehair and cotton, and discharged his excess energy into it on quiet afternoons. On one such occasion a spiral spring had given him a bad cut, which was slow to heal and left him with a scar on his glans. He called the dream-charged sofa his piggy bed. The Sash had no trouble at all in knocking it down. It went for a pair of fancy shoes. Only Bernd knew why he called them "piggy pumps."

His dreams had a specific object. Her name was Dr. Yvonne Geroldstein, who seemed to be about thirty. She seemed infinitely remote, light-years away, and not just because she belonged to the hated world of grown-ups. She taught history and "social studies." In both subjects Bernd was at the head of the class.

THE SURVIVOR

He crept to his new nest. His soul calculated. His instinct became yearning. The *Yuricke* had sunk, his father was dead, the Snail was gone, he had nothing more to offer the black market. That world of sordid trickery, criminal energy, cutthroat competition, and dark, cozy hideouts was gone from under him. To save himself, the swimmer had pushed off in another direction and gained access to two new worlds: the parsonage and Dr. Geroldstein's history class. He lived at the pastor's. At first the disgusting smell of clean bed linen prevented him from sleeping, and the regular hot meals laid him low. He lay in bed for whole days, the life gone out of him, his spirit broken, because food without a struggle, warmth without guile, a life without deception, thieving, and hairbreadth escapes disconnected all the circuits that had kept him going. Disused wires jangled inside him. The glorious bread dumplings in vanilla sauce at the parsonage filled his stomach but made him throw up. The pastor's tea instead of Kolya's vodka, a bed instead of a bumpy couch, a real breakfast instead of cold coffee. The pastor's wife fed the mangy stray dog without a word of comfort or explanation. It would just have to trickle into his system. The pastor gave him no sermons, no prayers, no maxims. Only books. Unbeknownst to Bernd, he had made inquiries at the school. He didn't get to the bottom of it, but he did learn Bernd's main interests: history and social sciences.

Bernd discovered new worlds. As a student the

pastor had worked in the Resistance. He had a large library; in addition to theology he had specialized in history and philosophy. Born in Brussels of German parents, Dr. Geroldstein had emigrated to London when Hitler came to power. There she had married a Jewish lawyer. That much was known at the school. Her husband — there were all sorts of rumors — was much older than she and was in poor health.

Like a turtle Bernd felt his way forward. Little by little his head emerged from his shell. This was a new coast, another continent where different, unaccustomed laws were in force. Here he found a new warmth that didn't have to be won by theft or trickery. At first the pastor's books were his planks. They exploded in his head, which up until then had been clogged with the clutter of the material world. Bernd had never thought, only reacted. His world had been his immediate environment, to be mastered by his energy. His knowledge of other people's worlds, play, and imagination went no further than *Sigismund Rüstig* or Karl May's *The Treasure in Silver Lake*. Now his scope expanded. He couldn't have said whether he had achieved something or whether it had come to him: something gentle, appealing, a new kind of pain. Caused by something rather than someone. He discovered something he had never known — no one had offered it to him and he had never been able to offer it to anyone: feeling. He didn't know what to do with it. Two currents were at work. His reading led to judgments. His father's study with its death mask, bayonets, and idiotic nude photos took on new contours. He came to see more behind it than meaningless obsessions; he saw that there was a world of retired major generals. Regardless of whether he read John Steinbeck or *The Communist Manifesto*, books were the key.

Books opened a passage through the wall between him and the surrounding world. He became vulnerable, because he was developing longings. He longed not only to have, but also to give. But what? And to whom? He had torn loose from his anchor, but had not yet found anything else to hold on to. Or grown a new skin. Instead, he resorted to all sorts of disguises. He went to American clubs where reeducation officers lectured about Erskine Caldwell or James T. Farrell; he saw Russian films at the Russian Cultural Center on Unter den Linden; he went — partly because he thought it chic — to the Maison de France on Kurfürstendamm and registered for a course on Cocteau, whose *La Belle et la Bête* he had seen three times. Those were the days of the blockade, and what was left of his black-market instincts brought him to Tempelhof Airport, especially at night. He was fascinated by the planes that landed every three minutes on the floodlit field, and there was always a possibility of swiping something or of earning five marks by phoning one of the newspapers when a plane missed the runway and landed in flames.

His old skin was molting. The new one was growing — or rather, a number of new skins were tried on like costumes. Boogie-woogie over cheap champagne — a children's production of Schiller's *Intrigue and Love* by the flickering light of gas lamps (the electricity functioned only at certain hours). Bernd was a big hit in the role of Wurm, he had put all his experience of human baseness and guile into it. A slimy character. None of these costumes fitted, they were all baggy, all were a part of his molting. In the school paper, which he himself edited, his affectations were heavy-handedly but aptly caricatured by one of his classmates in a report on a meeting of the student parliament: "A representative of the SED* camouflaged as an Independent asked for the floor. To judge by his dress, this SED spokesman might have been a member of the ultrafeudal bourgeoisie. It was ever so modern, in the American manner, his sand-colored double-breasted suit contrasted glaringly with the garb of the other members. And his ultramodern crepe-soled shoes aroused ironic admiration throughout the political spectrum. Amid cries of 'parlor Bolshevik,' 'kid-gloved proletarian,' he mounted the speaker's platform with a light swing-kid step. His speech was a critique of all four parties. Even with the SED, as he said, he was not in full agreement."

**Sozialistische Einheitspartei Deutschlands* (Socialist Unity Party). The official name for the Communist Party in East Germany.

His roles gave rise to mannerisms that could not yet have been termed attitudes. He had not yet come across the maxim "Knowledge is Power," but the reactions of the scurrying rat, which bit and stole and fought, developed into a form of eroticism. Bernd's eroticism was intellect, which he developed as a new means of survival. His mind was quicker now. "Let me finish!" he barked at a teacher who tried to shut him up when he went on at excessive length about Thomas Mann's *Dr. Faustus*, which none of the others had read. Thus a sensitive mind emerged from crepe-soled SED-spokesman Wurm. He had not yet heard of Freud or Marx, but he twined sex and Marxism together to form a bridge into life.

The car that called for Frau Dr. Geroldstein at noon had Russian license plates. Her husband worked in some scientific institute in the eastern sector. Bernd couldn't have said what fascinated him more: his discussions with her in class, which went on for hours to the bored indignation of his classmates, or the gangling nonchalance with which she stepped into the old BMW with the Soviet plates.

It was the perfume of the forbidden and unconventional. The pastor he chose as his guardian had aroused his enthusiasm by riding a bicycle, wearing short trousers, and lending him Tolstoy's *The Kreutzer Sonata* and a faded old linen-bound copy of Anna Seghers's *The Seventh Cross*. And this woman attracted him in very much the same way. She was as free from middle-class conventions as Irmchen, but she had gestures rather than affectations. Bernd began to follow her. He followed her car on his bicycle. And he was lucky — in the window of a photographer's shop near the Jannowitz Bridge he saw a big picture of her and her husband. He didn't understand why it should be there; he thought it must be an advertisement for the photographer, failing to realize that this was the eastern sector and that such a display had political significance. He went into the shop and asked: "Could you take my picture?" Inside there were two flashily dressed men, who said rather obsequiously: "Yes, of course. What sort of picture do you want?" Bernd had no idea. He hadn't planned his act. They sat him down in a chair and turned his head, which was wholly taken up with the picture in the window, this way and that. "We'd be glad to take a few more pictures of you," one of them said. He had never thought about himself, he was too much of an animal for that. He had no perception of his body and was quite unaware that he had become a handsome young man, whose reddish brown mop of hair contrasted pleasantly with his greenish eyes and dark complexion. He still had his unnecessarily long Coweye-lashes. "What kind of pictures?" "Come off it. You know what we mean. Anyway, not passport photos." Thanks to his business instinct he saw the possibilities of the situation. He wanted something, but the others had no way of knowing that what interested him was not pictures of himself but the photograph in the window. "It's your chance to make a bit of money." Now Bernd was at home, this was the world of black-market deals and exchanges. He didn't know exactly what they were up to, but he knew what to do. "OK. It's all the same to me what you want. But I want something too. I want the big photo in the window." It seemed somehow right to him that he should pay for it with his body. Bernd never called for the pictures that were snapped of him, some seated, some standing; he had had sense enough not to give them his address. He had no pictures of himself. But he had *the* picture. He cut the husband out of it. Not an act of aggression: he was just eliminating something irrelevant.

That same evening he crept to the little square where Dr. Geroldstein lived. There was a small waterless fountain in the middle with a bronze figure in it, which instead of feeding the fountain just stood openmouthed in a silent scream. Primulas were growing luxuriantly all around the fountain. Leaning against the bronze figure, he was able to observe the house in the twilight without himself being seen. He had no plans, he just wanted to stand there, stare at the windows, and watch shadowy figures moving behind the uncurtained windows. He bored his way into the house, but kept his eyes on the photo, which made him dizzy and faint. The picture, because he had it in his possession, was the real woman, more real than the teacher in the classroom or the married shadow in the house across the way. Strong and heavy and passionate came the realization: I want her. I want her life, I want to possess her, burst her open, fill her, flow into her. He began to lick the skin of his arms, to smell himself so as to taste her; only by knowing himself to the full would he be able to desire her with the tautness of a steel spring. He takes off his clothes as in the photographer's studio. Giving in order to possess. Soberly, his head full of a terrible clarity. His skin stretches as wide as the sea. A single great wave of feeling bathes him in salt and wetness, yet it is he himself. Wave and gullet, blood, snot, rose thorn, hair-matted wound that breaks open when he ejaculates, projects reddish-whitish stickiness, not into softness, and runs through thorns, down over his lacerated legs. He lays yellow, orange-rimmed petals on the gash and in a dream sets hands on it. His first night of love. In that imaginary encounter he experienced himself. Partnerless yearning.